Voices of Wom

Voices of Women from Afghanistan

Five Plays and the Stories that Inspired Them

Dancing to the Blast
Dust Allergy
Behind the Blast Wall
The Place of Shining Light
Parwana: They Bear All the Pain

Edited by
LESLEY FERRIS
with JENNY MORGAN

methuen | drama
LONDON • NEW YORK • OXFORD • NEW DELHI • SYDNEY

METHUEN DRAMA
Bloomsbury Publishing Plc
50 Bedford Square, London, WC1B 3DP, UK
1359 Broadway, New York, NY 10018, USA
29 Earlsfort Terrace, Dublin 2, D02 AY28, Ireland

BLOOMSBURY, METHUEN DRAMA and the Methuen Drama logo are trademarks of
Bloomsbury Publishing Plc

First published in Great Britain 2026

Design by Lara Himpelmann
Cover image by Stella Levi via Getty Images

A catalogue record for this book is available from the British Library.

A catalog record for this book is available from the Library of Congress.

ISBN: HB: 978-1-3505-4736-0
        PB: 978-1-3505-4735-3
        ePDF: 978-1-3505-4737-7
        eBook: 978-1-3505-4738-4

Series: Methuen Drama Play Collections

Typeset by RefineCatch Limited, Bungay, Suffolk
Printed and bound in Great Britain

For product safety related questions contact productsafety@bloomsbury.com.

To find out more about our authors and books visit www.bloomsbury.com
and sign up for our newsletters.

Contents

Illustrations

Acknowledgements

I would like to thank my former Ohio State University colleagues JiRye Lee, Melinda McClimans and Jeanine Thompson, and playwright and previous co-author Penny Farfan, for their care and attention in bringing this book together. To the playwrights I had the privilege of collaborating with and whose work is being published in this book, Nushin Arbabzadah, Alia Bano, Sonali Bhattacharyya, Monirah Hashemi and Yasmin Joseph, I am so grateful that we had this opportunity, and that you immediately saw the theatrical power of these Afghan women's stories. I would also like to thank the artist Arabella Dorfman and the photographer Joël van Houdt for allowing us to use their work in our signature image and in publicity material. Special thanks to Steve Harper at Theatre503 in London, theatremaker Valerie Kaneko-Lucas and producer and novelist Kate Sawyer. I am indebted to the journalist Zahra Joya, with whom I enjoyed many chats about her native Afghanistan. And of course none of this would have been possible without the encouragement of my husband Brian Rotman and our daughters, Amie and Phoebe Ferris-Rotman. To my editors, Sonali Chapman, who worked on an earlier draft with me, and to Jenny Morgan, who went above and beyond in making this anthology a reality, I thank you. And finally, to the Afghan female journalists who belonged to *Sahar Speaks*, thank you for telling your stories.

———

Introduction

Afghanistan was virtually unknown to me until my daughter, Amie Ferris-Rotman, went to Kabul to work as a senior correspondent with Reuters. During the height of President Barack Obama's troop surge in 2011,[1] she was struck by the fact that there were no Afghan women reporters working at any of the English-language media outlets in the country. This felt deeply hypocritical of the West, she thought, which had used women's rights to sell the war in Afghanistan to the public in the West,[2] and spent hundreds of billions of dollars on aid money directed at empowering Afghan women.

In 2014, Amie set up a training and mentoring scheme for women journalists, *Sahar Speaks*. The Afghan journalists who joined the programme began writing in English, and their work was first published in *The Huffington Post*.

I found their reports so striking that I commissioned women playwrights to bring the stories they told – about the unseen, mostly unknown, and often unexpected lives of girls and women in Afghanistan – to even more vivid life on the stage. In this anthology, we're publishing these five plays, making them available for the first time since they were performed to packed houses in the United Kingdom and the United States of America. We are also re-publishing the pieces of reportage that inspired them.

Why does the timing of this publication matter? The Taliban, the Islamist movement overthrown in 2001 by a military coalition led by the USA, returned to power in Afghanistan in 2021. It is now, once again, silencing Afghan women's voices. The oppression is so comprehensive that women are not even allowed to read the Qur'an aloud in the company of other women.

The journalism and the plays in this volume were produced during the two decades a Western-supported government was in power. Before it came crashing down in August 2021, the country was governed unevenly, and, as an Afghan-NATO coalition battled units of the Taliban, it was beset by violence. In 2013, playwright Nushin Arbabzadah observed that 'Afghanistan was an Islamic Republic and a democracy during the daytime, and in some parts, it became a Taliban-run Emirate with the sunset'.[3]

Did the decades when the Taliban was out of power close the gulf of inequality between men and women? They did not. Playwright and former child refugee Monirah Hashemi spent from 2004 to 2012 – her early adult years – in Afghanistan, battling to work independently as an actor, director and theatre producer. But in 2012 she went into exile again, because, she told me, 'During my eight years in Afghanistan, women's stories became the core of my work. But creating a female narrative did not come easy. The patriarchal society was not ready to hear from women, to listen to their stories. Society demanded that women keep silent about their own concerns and interests.'

The journalists we are publishing here did not keep silent about women's and girls' concerns. As MP Shukria Barakzai said, 'they shed light on dark corners where men can't'[4] – and their work was widely read.[5]

Now, none of these women journalists can write from Afghanistan. All have fled the country.

This anthology excavates their reports, and publishes the plays that imaginative playwrights spun from them, in the belief that readers and theatre-makers can make these women's words live again. As playwright Yasmin Joseph says, 'Given the current political climate, I think this is an incredibly powerful time to drown out the noise and listen to the people that society is constantly silencing or speaking over.'

From the page to the stage – how it happened

When Amie realised that none of the foreign media outlets reporting from Afghanistan employed Afghan women journalists, she was appalled. 'How can the world see the true Afghan story,' she asked, 'if there are no Afghan female writers, photographers, camera operators or TV producers at foreign news outlets? It would be more consistent for English-language media that produce numerous stories on women's rights to hire Afghan female reporters. This has been a *systemic failure* by the international press during one of the most important periods in Afghanistan's recent history.'[6]

One of the first pieces *Sahar Speaks* published in *The Huffington Post* was a blazing account by Zahra Joya, headlined 'I Dressed Like a Boy So I Could Go to School'.[7] Joya told me she didn't in fact speak English before she joined the course, but she refused to go away; she insisted on being given a chance. Her opening lines are a powerful introduction to a piece that shed light on dark corners: 'Life for an Afghan woman is gruelling,' she wrote, 'like a constant state of war. The country resembles a burning oven, where one can feel the heat of discrimination with every breath.'

I think live theatre is the art form of the present tense; it speaks to the heart and the body, as well as to the head. I believed we could turn Zahra Joya's story into a piece of theatre that would, in the urgent circumstances of the struggle in Afghanistan, help amplify the voices of

Sahar Speaks journalists share ideas for a story.
(*Photograph: Joël van Houdt, with kind permission*)

Afghan women and increase understanding of their situation. As one of our playwrights, Sonali Bhattacharyya, says: 'Stories allow us to imagine different ways of living, and that act of imagination is the first step to changing the world.'[8]

In the UK, I and my other daughter, Phoebe Ferris-Rotman, at the time an arts administrator and theatre producer, had established *Palindrome Productions*, a company inspired, we said, by 'the ability of the contemporary stage to make present histories that have been mislaid, erased or lost over time'. The stories the women journalists were writing documented histories that were in danger of being lost even as they happened.

Our first thought was to commission Afghan women playwrights; we rapidly discovered it was not so easy to find them. In the three years we worked on the theatre programme, we managed to commission two Afghan playwrights: Nushin Arbabzadah, who teaches on the West Coast of the United States, and Monirah Hashemi, who lives and works in Sweden.

We did not want to colonise the voices of Afghan women (an unfortunate strategy that took place throughout the NATO-led war at government, military and civil society levels). But we wanted to get started, so I asked Steve Harper, the literary manager at Theatre503 in London, for his advice.

We thought playwrights from a migrant or refugee background might tune in, not only to the text of the journalists' stories, but also to the many subtexts. After a number of interviews, we invited award-winning British playwrights Sonali Bhattacharyya, Yasmin Joseph and Alia Bano to write plays based on an individual story, with the added creative constraint that each piece would have to be maximum thirty minutes long, and could only have two female characters.

This volume demonstrates how our playwrights skilfully translated pieces of journalism into engrossing, lithe, sometimes funny, always revealing pieces of drama. Bhattacharyya describes how it took her time to find 'the dramatic heart of the story – the big, overarching theme' that lay beneath journalist Sparghai Basir Aryan's first-person accounts of her mother's and her own experiences (of university, work, dress, struggle). Bhattacharyya wanted, she says, 'not to give a verbatim account of the *Huffington Post* piece, but to be sensitive to the heart and subtext of Sparghai's writing.'

With minimal dramatic resources to aim for – two women actors on an unadorned stage for half an hour – these playwrights devised encounters that illuminate historical and social contexts while drawing us in to the feelings, hopes and painful disappointments of individual characters.

I started to pull this anthology together as Taliban forces were threatening to take power again. Several years on, girls are forbidden to go to secondary school and university; women are excluded from almost all employment. Public spaces – even parks – are forbidden to women. They can be beaten and arrested if they do not wear full body covering or allow their voices to be heard in public. Every day, Afghan women are being denied the freedom to live lives they might choose, to speak publicly, to write and publish, to participate openly in the social and cultural life of their country.

An international campaign is lobbying to have this recognised in international law as 'gender apartheid'.[9] The campaign has seen some progress: in January 2025 the prosecutor of the International Criminal Court announced he was seeking arrest warrants against the two most senior Taliban leaders 'for the crime against humanity of persecution by gender'.[10] Prosecutor Karim Khan said, 'My Office has concluded that these two Afghan nationals are criminally responsible for persecuting Afghan girls and women, as well as persons whom the Taliban perceived as not conforming with their ideological expectations of gender identity or expression [i.e. the LGBTQI+ community].'[11]

The five plays in this volume, and the news reports that inspired them, record voices that are now suffocated, the experiences of women that can't now easily be represented in any medium from within the country.[12] They

An animated journalism class, with *Sahar Speaks* founder Amie Ferris-Rotman at the desk.
(Photograph: Joël van Houdt, with kind permission)

open our eyes to the deep social currents that sweep Afghan women out of sight and into silence.

A note on theatre in Afghanistan

Music, poetry and story-telling have been practised for centuries by the ethnic and linguistic groups that make up the modern state of Afghanistan.[13] Playwright Alia Bano says, 'Often the citizens of Afghanistan are portrayed as uncultured – but this is not the case; there is a great oral tradition and love of stories in Afghanistan. Great writers such as Rumi and Ferdowsi have flourished when circumstances have allowed. That said, most writers today, such as the novelist Khaled Hosseini, have had to flee and find stability before they could weave their power with the pen.'

Nushin Arbabzadah says theatre has often featured one way and another in Afghan culture: 'From wandering Sadhu troops who performed epic tales of love in the narrow lanes and old bazaars of ancient towns to state-sponsored morality tales, the history of Afghan theatre,' she says, 'reflects the tragedy of a people in search of answers.'[14] Actors working with French director Corinne Jabar in 2005 to prepare a production of *Love's Labour's Lost* in Dari told her (somewhat ironically) that Afghanistan had 'only a short theatrical tradition . . . if one does not count the theatre erected by Alexander of Macedon when his army occupied parts of Afghanistan after 330 BCE . . .'[15]

In the more recent past, employing actors to perform scripted plays began around a hundred years ago, when a modernising king and queen, Amanullah and Soraya, built a Greek-style amphitheatre at their court outside Kabul and started putting on Shakespeare and Molière in Persian and Pashto. In the 1930s, a School of Fine Arts was founded in Kabul, and in the 1940s the government supported the creation of an Afghan National Theatre, based in Kabul.[16] (This theatre building was bombed when the Taliban first took Kabul in 1996; a documentary film made by French director Alexandra Paraboschi after the Taliban were overthrown in 2001 shows the dilapidated venue being brought enthusiastically back into use.[17])

But although physical theatres existed in the early twentieth century, until the 1950s, Afghanistan was like Elizabethan England – women were not allowed to perform. In 1955, a theatre company calling itself the Knowledgeable Women's Group established the Bahar Theatre and produced a range of productions that featured women on the stage. In the same year, the first drama school was established. The Parwan Youth Theatre opened in 1968, and in 1972 the Franco-Afghan Istiqlal High School was the first school to have its own theatre. The students' theatre group included girls from the Malalaï High School as well as boys from Istiqlal.[18]

But as Monirah Hashemi's experience suggests, Afghan women who wanted to write or perform theatre had to continue to battle social and religious conservatism. Paraboschi's film records joyful scenes at a theatre festival in Kabul in 2008, where 16 companies from the provinces performed plays, some about women's struggles, one where young women played male characters, and all where mainly male audiences were rapt, or laughed and clapped. But one young male performer tells Paraboschi he's had to challenge the preconceptions of his male friends that theatre is 'unwholesome'. For the women in the film, it's worse. Actress Shakiba Rezaï echoes Hashemi, that if a woman appears on a stage, most people think she's 'loose'.

A production of *Love's Labour's Lost* in Kabul in 2005 featured women alongside men. But Parwin, one of the women actors, was forced to leave her in-laws' house with her husband and their three children because his family was incensed that she had performed in public. Subsequently, Parwin's husband was kidnapped, and disappeared. She and her children fled to Pakistan, then to Canada.[19] 'Our people simply cannot accept women on the stage,' Parwin said in an interview in 2012, when she came to London to perform in a Dari-language production of *A Comedy of*

Errors, Afghanistan's entry in the Globe to Globe celebration for the World Shakespeare Festival.[20]

As an audience member at *Comedy of Errors,* I witnessed a full house, with many people standing in the yard at the Globe. As soon as the performance started, however, many Afghan men held up their phones and began recording. This was greatly worrying, considering that any images of the Afghan actresses might cause serious problems for them and their families in Afghanistan. Parwin made sure that at the end of the performance she and the other women actors covered their faces, to protect them at least in the vicinity of the theatre – though one performer said subsequently that she had received death threats and was afraid to go back to Afghanistan.[21]

The plays in this volume revolve around incidents of danger, abuse, misunderstanding, or systematic exploitation and oppression. But the playwrights always surprise us. In Hashemi's play, for instance, a thriller called *Dancing To The Blast,* the protagonists take a moment from contemplating their mortal plight to discuss purple nail polish and paint one woman's nails. Nushin Arbabzadah's tonally subtle play, *Dust Allergy*, is a comedy with elements of farce. Both Afghan playwrights offer glimpses of the brilliance and range that a regular theatre system in Afghanistan might produce if it was allowed to function.

As for the other three plays in the anthology – which are not written by Afghan women – one might ask how they can claim authenticity in a collection about Afghanistan. I argue they can because of the particular circumstances that inspired them: the playwrights read a published story by an Afghan woman journalist, and developed a play based on that specific story and its deeper themes (please read the playwrights' reflections and interviews after their plays later in this volume).

The writers we invited to contribute showed a particular sensibility. Bhattacharyya, for instance, says, 'I was struck by the honesty and bravery of the journalists, and was keen to be involved. I thought many of the pieces were ripe for a stage adaptation, especially as we don't see feisty, opinionated, educated and politicised Afghan women like this on UK stages, possibly any stages!'.

The stories the women journalists told, and the issues raised in the plays, haven't gone away just because the Taliban has pushed women back into obscurity. On the contrary.

I hope theatre-makers and educators at all levels will embrace these plays for their own merits, and give them further life. The power of these stories is crucial to us all. Why? Partly because the stories are embedded in a history many people in the West would rather forget – the deep involvement of the British Empire, and more recently the governments of

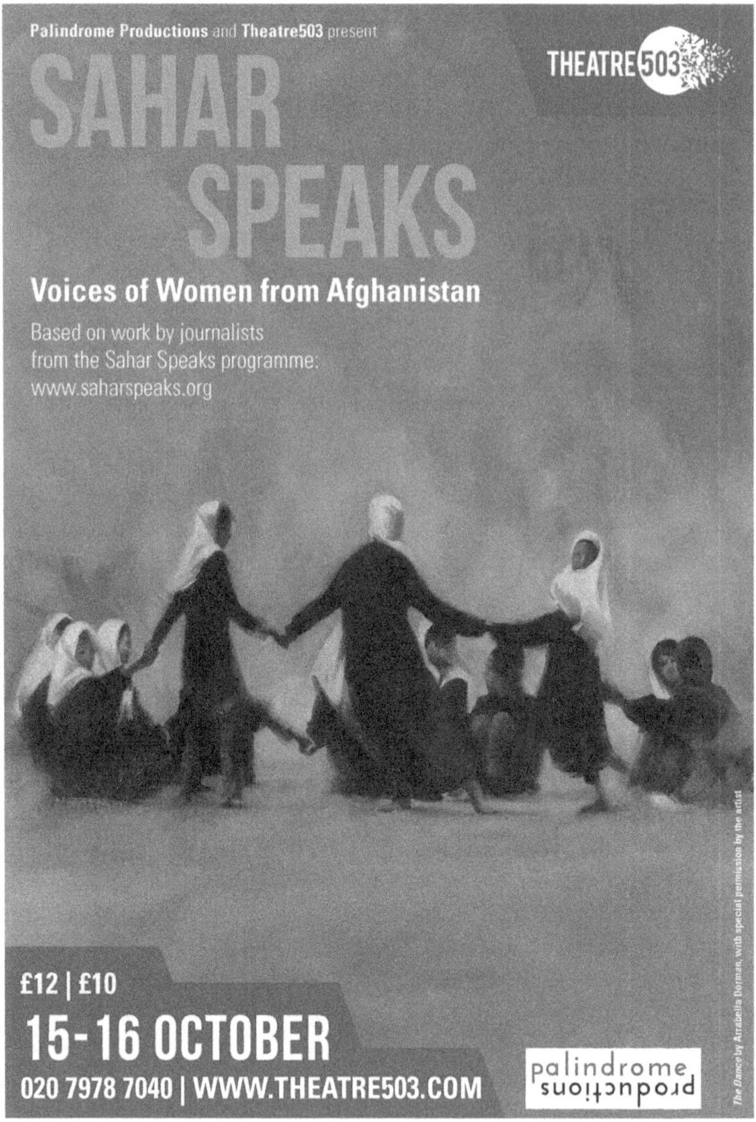

Poster for the first season of *Sahar Speaks* plays, at Theatre503, London,
October 2017.
*(Poster based on The Dance by Arabella Dorfman, by kind permission
of the artist)*

the UK and the US (amongst others), in Afghanistan's troubles (and theatre exists partly for the living to witness the past).

I look forward to seeing more Afghan plays by Afghan playwrights. They take us on a journey we rarely experience, but find fascinating when it happens. For instance, the stage adaptation of Khaled Hosseini's novel *The Kite Runner* ran (and re-ran) in the USA and the UK. Playwright Phil Porter's adaptation of Hamid Amiri's book, *The Boy with Two Hearts,* directed by Amit Sharma, broke audience hearts in Cardiff and on its transfer to the National Theatre in London. Afghan stories translated successfully into plays – they did what the work in our book does, and proved that audiences would come to see them.

Above all, I hope the plays and stories in this volume enable us to hear the voices of Afghan women. The Taliban may be stifling them, but their voices have not gone away.

Notes

1   For an account of what happened in the USA on 11 September 2001, and its aftermath, see, for instance, *September 11 attacks*, Peter L. Bergen, Britannica, https://www.britannica.com/event/September-11-attacks
2   See, for instance, *Report on the Taliban's War Against Women*, US Bureau of Democracy, Human Rights and Labor, 17 November 2001, https://2001-2009.state.gov/g/drl/rls/6185.htm
3   *Afghan Rumour Bazaar: Secret Sub-Cultures, Hidden Worlds and the Everyday Life of the Absurd*, Nushin Arbabzadah, Hurst & Company, London, 2013
4   http://www.saharspeaks.org/our-story
5   For some of the many successes the journalists achieved, see Amie Ferris-Rotman: https://www.huffpost.com/entry/sahar-speaks-afghan-women-journalists_n_59a7527ce4b0a8d145730b13
6   http://www.saharspeaks.org/our-story
7   'I Dressed like a Boy so I Could Go to School', Huffington Post, 21 June 2016, https://testkitchen.huffingtonpost.com/saharspeaks/#zahrajoya/
8   https://www.sonaliwrites.com
9   https://endgenderapartheid.today
10   https://www.opensocietyfoundations.org/newsroom/open-society-welcomes-step-toward-justice-for-afghan-women-and-girls
11   https://www.icc-cpi.int/news/statement-icc-prosecutor-karim-aa-khan-kc-applications-arrest-warrants-situation-afghanistan
12   See, for instance, director Sahra Mani's documentary film, produced by Jennifer Lawrence and Justine Ciarrocchi and executive produced by Malala Yousafzai, *Bread & Roses*, 2023: https://film-forward.com/documentary/bread-roses

13 See, for instance, Eliza Griswold and Seamus Murphy's book about *landays*, an improvised poetic couplet form practised in women's gatherings in eastern Afghanistan and western Pakistan: a 'vibrant, clandestine, and ancient tradition', says a reviewer. *I Am the Beggar of the World: Landays from Contemporary Afghanistan*, Eliza Griswold and Seamus Murphy, 2014

14 https://mesc.osu.edu/events/shakespeare-among-suicide-bombers-turmoil-theater-modern-afghanistan-nushin-arbabzadah

15 I am indebted to scholar Chin Min Edmund Chow for the information in his PhD thesis, *Afghan Theatres since 9/11: from and beyond Kabul*; Dissertation, University of Manchester, for a degree of Doctor of Philosophy in the Faculty of Humanities (2016); available here: https://pure.manchester.ac.uk/ws/portalfiles/portal/54588933/FULL_TEXT.PDF

16 Chow, *ibid.*

17 *Afghanistan: Reconstructing Through Theatre*, https://www.cultureunplugged.com/documentary/watch-online/play/5391/afghanistan-reconstructing-through-theatre

18 Alexandra Paraboschi's film has pictures of their productions, and an interview with Farida Raonaq, who was part of the student troupe: https://www.cultureunplugged.com/documentary/watch-online/play/5391/afghanistan-reconstructing-through-theatre

19 Chow, *ibid.*

20 Amie Ferris-Rotman, 'Shakespeare Gives Hope to Afghanistan Arts Revival', Reuters, June 6, 2012

21 Dr Edmund Chow, *Cultural Commodification of Afghanistan: A Case Study of 'The Comedy of Errors' in 2012 London Olympics*, 16 July 2019, https://www.researchgate.net/publication/334524087_Cultural_Commodification_of_Afghanistan_A_Case_Study_of_'The_Comedy_of_Errors'_in_2012_London_Olympics

Five plays, and the stories that inspired them

1

Dancing to the Blast

Monirah Hashemi

Adapted from a story by Pariwash Gouhari

We were delighted in 2018 when Monirah Hashemi, a multi-talented Afghan theatre-maker and performer based in Sweden, accepted our invitation to write a play based on a *Sahar Speaks/Huffington Post* report by Pariwash Gouhari.

The text of the Gouhari story is below, but please note that the online version of the report[1] includes a short film, shot and edited by Gouhari herself, where she interviews the two young women she describes in her piece, both of whom were disabled in their attempt to evade a Taliban attack. Since 2021, Gouhari has been working for the World Bank, based in the USA.

Afghan Women Long For Their Campus Life
A Year After Taliban Attack

Pariwash Gouhari, Sahar Speaks/Huffington Post, 31 August 2017

A year ago, the American University of Afghanistan was brutally attacked by the Taliban, leaving 13 dead and 30 injured. Two foreign professors, one from the United States and the other from Australia, were kidnapped and remain in Taliban captivity. The university, which gives scholarships to hundreds of women from all walks of life, was closed for seven months, with students dispersed back to provinces across the country.

Most of the students who were there during the attack are emotionally scarred. For women, especially those who were injured, their lives back home became suffocating and lonely.

I followed the journey of two women who suffered serious injuries when they jumped out of their second-floor classroom during the attack. Sultana Taib is in her second year of studying law; Soorya Azizi is a business administration major.

As Sultana leapt from the second floor, she fractured a bone in her back. She later found out that part of a bullet had also struck her back. The

23-year-old spends her days at home, reading books, drinking tea and watching movies to pass the time.

She says she misses her life in the dormitory, where she would regularly hang out with friends. She now stays in a rented flat in Kabul with her sister and communicates with her friends via her cellphone. She must deal with constant electricity outages and says she misses the steady generators the university provided for them.

Even though she is injured and at home, she still paints her nails, a small act of defiance against a society she says puts restrictions on women. She longs for the days when she can return to a normal life, and hang out with her university girlfriends in the cafes of Kabul, one of the few places where young women can meet and chat freely.

Nineteen-year-old Soorya broke her spine in a 30-foot-high fall. Initially, the doctors thought she would never walk again, but she has made steady progress, although she suffers enormous pain. In Afghan homes, friends and family usually sit on large, flat pillows called tushaks, and Soorya needs help to get up from the floor.

Like Sultana, she misses her friends and relishes their visits, even if they come by just for a cup of tea. She also loves to put on lipstick, as she would before going to classes, even though she spends her days at home with her family. She also spends time doing exercises. She tried to take an online class, but with Afghanistan's weak internet, it became nearly impossible.

The university reopened at the end of March, to jubilation from the students.

As originally featured in The Huffington Post

MONIRAH HASHEMI

Playwright, performer

Hashemi was born into an Afghan refugee family in Iran, but when she was 18, after the first Taliban government had been deposed, her family returned to Herat, in western Afghanistan. There, she told me, 'despite strong opposition from the heads of my family – my father and grandfather – I decided to be an actor. Soon, sexual harassment from colleagues began. A woman who chooses to stand before a male audience, before cameras or on the stage, is a representation of guilt and depravity. She is considered a loose woman, a prostitute.'

Nonetheless, Hashemi co-founded a production company, the Simorgh Film Association of Culture and Art. At 21, she wrote and directed her debut play, *Cry of History*, which was performed to a mixed audience in Herat at the country's first educational theatre festival in 2006. Her many other theatre credits include *Masks under the Burka*, which was selected for the Thirteenth Black Sea International Theatre Festival in Turkey, and performed at the Women's International Playwright Conference in Stockholm in 2012. She says about working in Afghanistan, 'Being a female artist meant nothing but absolute censorship. We had to compromise day and night, deceive ourselves about our feelings and emotions, manipulate our thoughts and beliefs to survive. Though we were surrounded by taboos, rules, demands, conventions, injustices, and long-time structural silence, we worked to send out our voice and our stories.'

Living in asylum in Sweden, Hashemi's creative activity[2] includes film work, writing, directing, performing, and cultural interventions in Malmö like *Nights with Buddha*, which evoke the statues of the Buddha in Bamiyan that the Taliban blew up in 2001 – 'a deliberate act of cultural genocide', she calls this; the *Nights* are, she says, 'an artistic act of resistance'.[3]

Hashemi came to London for rehearsals for the staged reading of *Dancing to the Blast*, delivered a lecture, 'Women: Taboos of Stage and Stories',[4] and performed excerpts from *Cry of History*.

DANCING TO THE BLAST: SYNOPSIS

Students Yagana and Zeba are in an upstairs corridor at the American University of Afghanistan, waiting for an evening class to begin, and Zeba is teasing Yagana about a young man, singing a provocative song. As they're laughing, there's a blast that throws them to the floor, and the lights go off. They rush into a classroom, and spot a gunman in the courtyard below; he sees them and fires, shattering the glass of the window. They try to block the door with desks, and as they're contemplating their possible fate, Zeba gives Yagana the purple nail polish she's bought for her. They drop their bags out of the window, and as the door is shoved open, they're standing on the window-frame, holding hands. Blackout. The original Pariwash Gouhari report located the two young women, who had jumped but survived, and were disabled. Hashemi leaves the outcome open.

Dancing To The Blast

Monirah Hashemi

Completed and © May 2018
Rehearsed reading 16 July 2018 at Camden People's Theatre, London

Actors: Rasheeda Ali, Mona Khalili
Director: Rachel Valentine-Smith

Characters

Yagana *a 22-year-old girl, friendly but serious, in her second year at university. She is dressed in dark brown, wears a green shawl and carries a green bag.*

Zeba *20, in her first year at university. She is a happy, loud and funny girl. She is dressed in yellow and blue, and has red lipstick and red nail polish.*

Setting

A corridor and a class room at the American University of Afghanistan

Time

August 2016

Scene One

AT RISE: Spotlight on a closed door, downstage centre.

The play begins behind the door of a classroom.

The time is a few minutes before 7pm.

Zeba *has followed* **Yagana** *to her class.*

It's early, and no-one else has arrived yet.

We hear their discussion but don't see them.

Yagana   This is not the right time. Stop doing this! They'll be here any minute.

Zeba   It won't take much time. Just listen! You'll hear it!

Yagana   There's nothing but silence.

Zeba   That's exactly what you need to listen to. You'll hear it through the silence. I've done it many times myself. I know it works.

Yagana   It's stupid. You should be going now. They're coming, I can hear them.

Zeba   Wait! Wait! Don't push me, I'll go. But, but before I go, just try for once. Please.

Yagana *sighs heavily.* **Zeba** *gets excited*

Thank you. Ok, come! Sit here, on this chair! Good. Close your eyes. Concentrate. Focus on the chair beneath you and try to feel the energy that exists within it! Do you feel anything? Ah, great! Name the energy with an emotion that describes it. Keep it to yourself. Don't reveal it to me. Ok! Fantastic. Sit on this chair now! Same thing again. Close your eyes. Focus. Feel the energy and find a related emotion for it. *(Silence)* You see! Every chair has a special energy and emotion. And if you pay extra attention, you find connections between them. Tell me, whose chair is this?

Yagana (*bored*)   I think Wahid sits on it.

Zeba   From my experience and personal research, which are one hundred percent true, I can say: Wahid is deeply in love with the person sitting on that chair.

Yagana   And that's my chair, stupid!

Zeba   And how do you know Wahid is not in love with you?

Yagana   Nonsense. I'm done. Go and do your personal research in your own class! The students will be here any minute. I don't want them to witness this embarrassment.

Zeba *opens the door.*

Zeba   I can't see anyone in the corridor. Are you sure it's students plural and not a particular student who is coming?!

Zeba *starts singing in Dari.*

زَنُم ناله که نالهِم نالهبَر نیست

زَنُم ناله کِه دلبر را خبر نیست

Yagana   Shush!

Zeba (*still singing*)

زَنُم ناله بَه درگاهِ اِلهی

مِگر آهِ دلِ مُو کارگر نیست

Yagana   I said shush!

Yagana *appears by the door. She softly pushes* **Zeba** *to the side and checks the corridor.* **Zeba** *dances and continues singing.*

Zeba

زمین نَرم رَ مالَه گُنُم مُو

آخ ز دردِ عاشقی نالَه گُنُم مُو

همه میگَن که تَرکِ یار خود کُو

چطُو تَرکِ گُلِ لالَه گُنُم مُو؟

Yagana   *Starts to leave*

I don't care who says what, but I don't want to hear this silly nonsense ever again. Not from you, not from any of our girls.

Zeba   *Following her*

Can he talk to you then?

Yagana   *Stops in the corridor*

I think instead of worrying about every bee (*holds Zeba's nose with her two fingers*), I need to take care of the hive itself.

Zeba   *Teasing her*

Please, be nice to him. Don't be mean, ok? He is just a lover who's in love with the wrong girl.

Yagana   What?! What do you mean, wrong girl?! What is wrong with me?

Zeba   Just give him a chance to talk to you. Don't compare him with the others, those IDIOTS. At least he won't make trouble, even if you reject him.

Yagana   Keep your voice down! Someone might hear.

Zeba   *Gestures as a herald*

Hear ye! Hear ye! (*Points to herself.*) You are looking at a bridesmaid-to-be. . . . very soon.

Yagana   That's enough.

Zeba   Ok, ok. You may have some prince in your mind, a mandil dude⁵, but I really want Wahid to be my best friend's . . .

Yagana   *Interrupts*; hugs **Zeba** *and they both laugh*

Stop this nonsense! Promise me!

Zeba   What nonsense? I have the right to dream.

Yagana   Dreams are private and personal. Dream for yourself!

Zeba   That's what I'm doing. Dreaming of a peaceful country, where I'm a lawyer and of course a bridesmaid as well.

Both laugh. **Yagana** *tries to stop* **Zeba** *from talking by covering her mouth. As they roar with laughter louder and louder, a powerful blast is heard. The lights go off.*

For few seconds, a deep silence spreads over the room. Then the space is filled with the ringing and buzzing in **Yagana** *and* **Zeba**'s *ears and heads.*

Succession of power outages. Between each, we see **Zeba** *and* **Yagana** *dancing on and off, as if their bodies are floating amidst the noises. Choreographed intervals start and end with both of them on the floor.*

Zeba   What was that? What happened?

No response from **Yagana**

Are you ok?

Zeba *tries to get her on her feet*

Let's get out of here.

Zeba *leads* **Yagana** *towards the exit.* **Yagana** *holds her hand and refuses to go, shaking her head. Gun fire from stage right, the direction* **Zeba** *was heading to.* **Yagana** *points to the classroom and they run towards it.*

As they reach the door, they push it upstage centre, turn with it and once they are hidden by the door, they rush through it into the classroom.

Scene Two

Zeba *and* **Yagana** *lean on the door, standing and breathing heavily.*

Stage right, a table and a chair behind it. Opposite them, some desks arranged in neat rows.

Sounds of gunfire. **Zeba** *holds on to* **Yagana**. **Yagana** *rushes to the window upstage right and* **Zeba** *to the window upstage left; they push them downstage right and left and look outside.*

The window upstage right is open and the other one is closed. **Zeba** *tries to open it but does not succeed. She joins* **Yagana** *at the other window.*

Zeba   *With panic*

Are we under attack?!

Yagana   It seems so.

Zeba   Are we going to die?

Yagana   I have no intention to die here and I won't let you either.

Zeba   Few people have survived indoor attacks.

Yagana   I won't give them the joy of killing us.

Zeba   These Bags of Feces! Why they are so intent on killing people? Why. . . .

Yagana   *Interrupts*

Come and help!

She locks the door and they start blocking it with desks and chairs.

Yagana   We won't make it if we get out through that door, or if we stay in here.

Goes to the opened window and looks outside.

Shit!

Zeba   *Joins Yagana and looks down*

Yeah, those cement blocks! Of course, we could choose to break our necks . . .

Angrily leaves the window

You are out of your mind if you think I will jump from here.

She takes lipstick out of her bag and puts it on her lips.

Yagana   You prefer a bullet!

Zeba   Anything that does not make me suffer.

Yagana   And you can cope with the torment of waiting until it's your turn?

She drags a chair to the window. Stands on it and sticks the upper part of her body out to examine the ground under the other window.

Zeba   They will be sent to hell long before they even get to this floor.

Yagana   You know fully well that most indoor attacks have lasted 7 hours, at least.

She moves to the other window and tries to open it.

There is a chance to be saved if we could only open this bloody window!

Zeba   Every day, the maniac Ashraf Ghani[6] increases security around his palace to save his own ass, and then he calls these Bags of Feces "The Dissatisfied / Angry Brothers". If these are his brothers, then for God's sake why they don't sit together to solve their family problems?

Yagana   *Tries to open the window*

Keep your voice down! You know full well that these brothers of Ghani hate to hear women's voices, especially those who curse.

Zeba   And YOU should know I've never let that stop me.

Yagana   I know, you've always been the wild one. But please, please understand we need to bow low right now. These gunmen's power is a legacy of blood. The power of their families is a legacy of blood. In the middle of their war, you and I are NOTHING. If they kill us today, it won't even be regarded as a crime. It'll only be seen as a result of their *dissatisfaction*. Who cares about what the President has said or done right now, we're just in the middle of these brothers' fight, and if you doubt they'll get to us on this floor, then I have to be reasonable for both of us . . . once again.

Pulls the handle of the window

It doesn't open!

Zeba   Why you are trying to scare me?

Yagana   *Moves towards* **Zeba**

I'm trying to save us. Both of us. Trust me.

Goes back to the window and looks outside

It's clear under this window. But it won't open. It's stuck.

As she looks outside, she sees someone.

There's a person out there.

Zeba   Let's stay inside.

Yagana   He has a gun.

Zeba   It's safer in here.

Yagana   He's looking at me.

Zeba   Maybe he is a policeman?

She runs towards the window.

Yagana   *Grabs* **Zeba**

Get on the floor!

They throw themselves on the floor. Gunfire erupts. The window shatters.

Yagana   No, it's not safe and he's not a policeman. He shot at me.

Looks at the window

On the bright side, he's opened the goddamn window.

Zeba   Unfair competition! He's got a gun! Of course he could open the window. I've never needed one . . . in the history of my life, no window has ever survived my sling shot attacks.

Yagana *checks outside carefully. Then she runs towards the table. She drags it and places it under the window. She steps on it and removes the remaining glass from the window frame.*

Yagana   Come!

No response from **Zeba**

He knows we're here and he's coming for us.

No response

Nothing would make him happier than killing two young women with no burqa, studying at the American University.

Gun fire erupts from a closer range. **Zeba** *runs to* **Yagana**

They're not shooting in the air. It's innocent people they're aiming at. Every gunshot means someone might be dying in fear and silence. Get up!

Zeba *jumps on the table.* **Yagana** *stands by the window frame and looks down. She turns, looks at* **Zeba** *and moves away.*

Yagana   You go first!

Zeba   I can't.

Puts lipstick on

I can't.

Yagana   Yes, you can!

Zeba   *Puts lipstick on again*

You go first.

Yagana   I'm not going anywhere before I'm sure you're safe.

Zeba   I can't. I can't jump.

Yagana   Don't think of it as jumping. Think of it as flying.

Zeba   I'm not a kid you're putting to sleep with stories of princes and fairies. We're going to die!

Yagana   Death, in all its certainties, is still only a possibility, and will remain so until our very last breath. No one can save one but oneself. You and I must struggle till our last drop of blood to survive.

Zeba   What is the point of fighting back when death is certain?

Yagana   People die when hope dies in them. You and I will survive. Our lives might change, but we will live. We will see our families again, our friends, and drink green tea with Shir pera[7] in Kabul cafes. We'll graduate from university and you'll be the successful lawyer you have always dreamed of. You and I will go and buy that purple lipstick and nail polish you chose for me.

Zeba *opens her bag and hands a small box to* **Yagana**.

Zeba   I already got them for you.

Yagana   *Hugs her*

You've always been so timely my dear.

She sits on the left side of the window.

Yagana   Come! Sit with me.

Zeba *joins her and sits on the right side*

Do you remember my cousin? The one you met at my brother's wedding. You said she seemed upset with you! How did you know that?

Zeba   From ERC!

Yagana   What is that?!

Zeba   My Energy Research Chair!

Yagana   *Opens the box, gives it to* **Zeba***. Gives her left hand to* **Zeba***, who starts putting purple nail polish on it.*

When I was a child, I used to live in a village with my family. We had a big house on two floors. My room was on the second floor. But I loved to play downstairs in the kitchen, where the window had a very deep niche. Sometimes I would lie there for hours, looking at the big garden, its flowers, trees and the many animals we had: ducks and geese, their babies, a rooster, hens and chickens, turkeys, a dog, and goats, and sheep. Many times, I used to sleep there.

One day, my cousin Razi visited us from the city. She's six months older than me. As children, we were not allowed to wear makeup. It was forbidden. But that day we sneaked into my mum's room and put on lipstick and nail polish.

Zeba *finishes the left hand and starts with the right hand.*

That day we played downstairs, by the kitchen window. In the middle of our game, we started fighting over a doll. Though Razi was older and physically stronger than me, I was a tough girl as well. She pushed me through the window. And I instantly grabbed her by the hair.

I was hanging from it, trying to keep myself from falling down. Razi was screaming: let my hair go! And I kept saying: I can't. I'll die. I heard my mum running towards us. She was shocked. She stood beside me and said: let go of her hair!

I said: No, I won't. I'll die.

She took hold of my hands and whispered in my ear: stretch your leg.

I refused. She repeated: stretch your leg. And I did it. I stretched my leg, and it touched the ground. When I was pushed out of the window, I was convinced I was on the second floor.

Zeba *puts purple lipstick on* **Yagana***.*

Razi never visited us again. When we get out of here, I will visit her and ask her to forgive me. We could have been good friends. We could have had a different relationship had our fears, our silence, our judgments, not stood in the way; had our hope for forgiveness allowed us to reach out to one another.

Zeba   *She hands the lipstick and nail polish back to* **Yagana***.*

Great things are not easily obtained.

Yagana   Especially life. Life needs courage. It needs hope.

Zeba   And a strong will to carry on with it.

Yagana   *Puts the box back in her bag. Holds both her and* **Zeba***'s bags, opens her arms and let the bags fall down.*

Looking down

That's where we're going to land. Will you sing before we fly?

Zeba

مَزَن یار یار که یارت خواهد آمد
به دل صبر و قرارت خواهد آمد
مَزَن یار یار، مَنال اِقذر شُو و روز
کِه یار آخر کِنارت خواهد آمد

A man is heard outside, followed by gunfire. He pushes the door and hits it with the gun. **Yagana** *and* **Zeba** *hold each other's hands.*

BLACKOUT

A gunshot is heard.

––––––––––––––––

Reflections from playwright Monirah Hashemi

Early in 2021 I began posting videos on my social media where I appeared in a white turban and a black Abā – a piece of lace under a see-through clerical cloak – and recited verses from the Qur'an. These verses were not chosen randomly. Rather, their content and message were the most important point. In a society where sex and sexuality are taboo and homosexuality punishable by death, the content of the verses offers Huri and Qelmān – virgins and beautiful young boys – in the promised paradise; merely sexual instruments for those who enter paradise: the men.

Soon, the videos went viral. My writing and visual work were attacked by social media users. I was tagged and mentioned in different chat groups under the names of Pro-Taliban and others; these were groups with thousands of followers. My Facebook and Instagram accounts, photos and videos were tagged with the following demands: 'Every true Muslim who sees and reads this post is obliged to report her social media pages'; 'Every true Muslim has a duty to remember her face and kill her in appropriate circumstances.'

To many people my actions might seem extreme. But when it comes to social change, we all need to play our role and do our part so that we can bring the slightest change in the culture and society we live in. To do that, we choose different mediums, platforms, tools, contexts, media, forms, and modes of expression. Some choose to activate within the defined frameworks that are in line with socially accepted norms, and some go beyond social beliefs and conventions.

Change does not come by itself. We need to foster it by generating dialogue and conversation. We must challenge society and its social norms, beliefs, and organizations. We need to address, point out, and highlight questionable issues that stand at the core of social injustices and women's oppression.

As an artist, specifically a female artist, whose background is from one of the most traditional societies in the world, one of my concerns has always been the narration of women's stories and experiences in the patriarchal, highly traditional and conservative religious perspective. Despite all obstacles I have always considered it my duty to push against conventions and limits, and challenge society to reflect on those boundaries.

Being born into a very religious and conservative family, my early questions were: who speaks and what do they say? Why do women have no control of the retelling of their lived experiences and no rights in giving voice to their feelings? I clearly remember when my mother was telling stories from her childhood my father would constantly interrupt her to correct her, even though their childhoods were spent in different countries. I was wondering all the time, who and what gives him the right and authority to put himself in the centre of truth, to deny my mother's experience and correct her memories?

The act of remembering and forgetting is not personal. In every society where women's existence is bound by the family's honour, their hopes and dreams are taken hostage by the patriarchal system. In such contexts, the socio-political structures impose certain forms of remembrance and forgetting.

Unfortunately, no society is free from the idea of supremacy and privilege provided for specific groups and classes. Such a system has no trouble labelling many as inferior. Male supremacy encourages the subordinate status of women by manipulating the definition of freedom and violence.

These days I live in terror. I can't even imagine the experiences of young girls who now face the return of the Taliban. Their schools are shut down. Their personal lifestyle is denied. They cannot discuss their experiences and share them with friends. I keep asking myself, what can I do? What can I do as a woman, as an artist and as a Hazara?[8]

My new performance, *Who Lights the Stars?*,[9] is my personal narrative. My story is true for many who are living under a system of oppression and silencing. To bring a transformation we need to refer to ourselves and begin from there. In order to make a male-controlled society develop both tolerance and awareness of women's narratives, we need to make them listen, to see and acknowledge women's suffering.

Monirah Hashemi rehearsing *Who Lights the Stars?* for the Folkteatern, Järnet in Karlstad, Sweden, October 2020.
(Photograph: Sara Svärdsén, with kind permission)

Who Lights the Stars? is my contribution towards a change for women all around the world, not only in Afghanistan. Every story is unique, important, worthy of being told by its storyteller. Though we live in the 21st century, the world is still dark, ignorant of women's suffering. In this darkness, every story and storyteller is a star, and we need countless storytellers to light the dark sky above us.

Notes

1   https://www.huffpost.com/entry/afghanistan-women-students-taliban-attack _n_598c7518e4b0d793738d2499
2   Monirah Hashemi's website is a rich source of information about her work: https://monirahhashemi.com/
3   https://monirahhashemi.com/2024
4   https://www.palindromeproductions.org/women-taboos-of-stage-and-stories
5   A rich, well-dressed man
6   Ashraf Ghani was president of Afghanistan from 2014. On the day the Taliban were on the outskirts of Kabul, 15 August 2021, he fled the country; hours later, the Taliban had themselves filmed in the presidential palace.
7   An Afghan sweet made with milk, rosewater, walnuts, pistachios and cardamom
8   See https://www.britannica.com/topic/Hazara
9   https://monirahhashemi.com/the-tale-of-the-stars

2

Dust Allergy

Nushin Arbabzadah

Adapted from a story by Fariba Housaini

After Nushin Arbabzadah's father smuggled the family out of Afghanistan in 1988, she went to school and university in Germany and England, became a professional translator from German, Persian and Spanish, and currently works as a lecturer in the Department of Communication at UCLA in Los Angeles.[1]

She was, we thought, the obvious person to adapt Fariba Housaini's piece for the stage.

Housaini graduated from the Asian University for Women in Bangladesh with a degree in Politics, Philosophy and Economics, and before she joined *Sahar Speaks* had a fellowship at the Ministry of Counter Narcotics in Kabul.[2]

Afghan Students Who Studied Abroad Are Hit With Reverse Culture Shock

Fariba Housaini, Sahar Speaks/Huffington Post, 31 August 2017[3]

Several years ago, Anita Haidary returned to her home country of Afghanistan after studying for a degree at Mount Holyoke College in Massachusetts.

"The homeless people on the street moved me in ways that I was not used to," she told me of her return as we sat in front of a large window on the second floor of a coffee shop. The crisp Afghan winter sun is shining on us. Though she has a rewarding job as a national policy consultant at the World Food Program, she is constantly reminded of the hurdle of being a woman in her native Afghanistan.

"For two weeks I didn't want to go out, it was so horrible," she said, detailing the widespread street harassment that plagues Afghan women's everyday life. "They invade your personal space and privacy, telling you that you need to wear this or that, or need to lose weight. It was so shocking."

Reverse culture shock is a growing problem for the Afghan elite who study abroad but must return once their education has finished. Returning home is often difficult, whether it's getting used to the garbage, pollution and child street beggars, or the renewed violence that is sweeping the country.

After returning home, Afghan returnees miss their international friends, memories, classroom environment, being able to go to parties, have fun, and experience new cultures and festivals. They could dress the way they wanted and walk freely through the streets without harassment, even at night.

Aalam Gul Farhad, 27, who studied political science at the American University of Central Asia in Kyrgyzstan, said she had forgotten how the constant blaring of car horns in Kabul could sound. She returned to Kabul two years ago. In Bishkek, she rode in cars on neatly paved roads and was almost never harassed by male passersby. "The drivers use their horn for nothing here! Even if a girl is walking to the other side of the street, they just keep beeping it. It's so irritating!"

Reverse culture shock does not only apply to women.

When Nasrullah Hussaini first returned to Kabul two years ago from India, where he studied engineering, he missed his independence and the solitude he had enjoyed. In Kabul, he is constantly surrounded by his large extended family, with whom he lives. Being educated abroad has given the 23-year-old respect, he noted, saying that locals come to him and ask him to weigh in on disputes and decisions. "I try to not let them down," he said.

Mohammad Hussain Bigzad, 25, who studied for five years at Mongolia's International University, found himself defending his actions when people assumed his faith had changed while abroad, asking him if he had picked up a girlfriend or if he fasted during Ramadan.

"I thought they'd have questions about my education, but instead they were just interested in seeing what had changed in me, looking for negative things."

Some of the returnees face depression and a disjointed sense of displacement. "I was struggling with how to deal with the dual expectation of myself versus the reality of the situation in Kabul," Haidary said.

While men are often revered when they come home after studying abroad, women can be viewed with suspicion in the deeply patriarchal society. Getting used to wearing a hijab again has taken some time, she said, and she needs to be more careful in the way she dresses when she visits her relatives.

When Haidary first returned, she said, she could hear locals whispering about her, "Dokhtar Americayee shoda" ("the girl has become Americanized"), which does not have particularly positive connotations.

Farhad said she needed to explain to other Afghan women why she was acting the way she did, and she tried to challenge the social norms. Luckily, her father is well-respected in their community, and she was able to secure a job as a program officer in the Afghanistan Institute for Civil Society, a nongovernmental organization.

Not all students struggle, though. Zahra Ghulami, 26, was given the opportunity to stay on after earning her bachelor's degree from the National University of Mongolia, but patriotism and missing her family won against the possibility of escaping war. "It was not as difficult as I thought, and after only a few weeks of staying at home, I found a job very quickly." She now works as a researcher in public policy.

If these students had studied in Afghanistan, they know their lives would be remarkably different. For the women, they say they would most likely be married by now and already have children. But seeing a world away from the conservative Afghan viewpoints made them grow into more interesting people, they say. Now they hope to use their experiences to improve their country, in both their private and public lives.

As originally featured in The Huffington Post

NUSHIN ARBABZADAH

Playwright

'When I lived in Kabul,' says playwright, writer and journalist Nushin Arbabzadah, 'I was a run of the mill "good Afghan girl" – shy and submissive . . . If you were a girl, you aspired to becoming the human equivalent of a baby rabbit – a mammal born with closed ears and eyes.'[4]

Arbabzadah grew up under Soviet occupation in Afghanistan, but when her father found himself inadvertently on the regime's black list, the family fled. After school in Germany, Arbabzadah gained a Master's degree in German and Spanish Literature and Linguistics at Hamburg University; in England, she gained an M.Phil. in Oriental Studies at

Pembroke College, Cambridge and worked for the British Council and the BBC; currently she works at UCLA.

Through all these achievements, Arbabzadah struggled against her 'baby rabbit' conditioning. It took her, she says, 'a long time and much battle with the Afghan community to change and become an individual.' In her collection of essays, *Afghan Rumour Bazaar*, she says, 'My survival instinct sent me to a Maoist-style cultural re-education camp made all by myself. I learned to look men and women in the eye, keep my head high, and argue my point ... I became angry and vocal; educated and self-confident; qualities in women regarded in Afghanistan most of the time with contempt and suspicion.'

In Autumn 2019, for Ohio State University in Columbus, colleagues and I raised funding for a multi-media series of events under the title 'On the Front Lines: Performing Afghanistan'.[5] Arbabzadah's *Dust Allergy* was premiered as part of the season, but some months before that she delivered the Lawrence and Lee Theatre Research Institute Annual Lecture, 'Shakespeare Among the Suicide Bombers: The Turmoil of Modern Afghan Theatre'.[6]

In *Dust Allergy*, Arbabzadah translates difficulties into comedy and farce – 'A Theatre of Tricksters', she calls it, in her Afterword to the play.

DUST ALLERGY: SYNOPSIS

In the sitting-room of a middle-class family home in Kabul, 19-year-old Arzo, whose T-shirt reads 'Be Yourself', is ignoring her mother Zohra's questions while a puppy yaps in the background; 'just my computer', says Arzo, but it soon becomes clear it is not. Arzo has returned from a year studying in the US, and her mother is keen for her to find a good job; but Arzo can hardly bear to go outside. 'You must stop hiding like a mouse in a trap', says Zohra. 'See, you don't understand,' says Arzo, 'You're too Afghan to understand.' Several scams and teases later, and a wind-up about Zohra's new boss filming Arzo's rescue of the puppy as a prime example of how not to behave in Afghan culture – something 'foreign Afghans' like Arzo get wrong – all expertly knitted together as tragicomedy and farce, everything works out fine.

Dust Allergy

Nushin Arbabzadah

Completed and © 16 August 2019
Performed 7 October 2019 at Ohio State University, Columbus, Ohio

Actors: Mehek Sheikh, Jordan Booker
Director: Rina Hajra

Characters

Arzo   *a young Afghan woman, around 19 years old.*
Zohra   *Arzo's mother. Middle-aged.*
Mrs. Malik   *landlady. Similar age to Arzo's mother.*

Setting

Kabul/ Afghanistan. Sitting-room of a middle-class Afghan family.

AT RISE: Arzo, *a 19 year old Afghan girl who wears a t-shirt with the slogan 'Be Yourself', is coughing while dusting. Her mother,* **Zohra**, *has just walked into their home from work. In the background, there's the intermittent sound of a yapping puppy.*

Arzo   You're late, mother. I've been worried.

Zohra   Arzo, what did you do today?

Arzo   *Coughs*

Honestly mother, I can't breathe. You're so covered in dust.

Zohra   I know the game you are playing, Arzo, I wasn't born yesterday. You ignore my question and then cough and hope that I'd get distracted and move on.

Pause

But let me tell you my child, your mother hasn't moved on an inch. Your mother is glued to the spot. So, here it is again, my question. What did you do today, Arzo?

Arzo   Why do you ask, mother?

Zohra   Oh, how clever she is, my daughter. Answers my question with her own question. Fine. Let me ask another question. Is there a reason why I shouldn't ask what you did today?

Arzo   What's this look, mother? You are frightening me.

Zohra   But can't you hear it?

Arzo   Hear what?

Zohra   There's a dog barking.

Arzo   It's not a dog barking. It's a puppy yapping and don't worry, that's just my computer, okay?

Zohra   I feel like a ship that's about to sink. Can you imagine a dog inside a Muslim house?

Arzo   It's just the computer, mother. It's not real.

Zohra   Thank god for that. Just imagine, a filthy beast in the house and today of all days and at this hour of all the hours.

Arzo   Why today of all days?

Zohra   Come here, come closer, let me take a look at you.

Arzo   No, mother, not now, please.

Zohra   Why not? Because you don't want me to see. But I do see. You look so pale, as if you've seen a ghost. Why are you so pale? Do you have something to confess?

Arzo   Can I have some privacy, please? How many times do I have to repeat, I need space; I need privacy, oh my god.

Zohra   But I need to know. I am worried.

Arzo   It's the jetlag! There's your answer.

Zohra   I asked Barbara and you know what she said? No jetlag after a month and that includes the likes of you, those who come from America.

Arzo   What if I am not like other people? What if I am different? Actually, everyone's different, that's what people here don't understand. Everyone's different.

Zohra   Trust me, they do understand. If anything, they understand too well. They think you've come back from America too thin. That's why you are hiding.

Arzo   Too thin? Last week it was too fat.

Zohra   They think that's why you are hiding in the house and not coming out.

Arzo   Oh my god! Why can't they just leave me alone, let me be myself? Look at my t-shirt. It says 'Be Yourself'. I have to wear it every day and look at myself in the mirror and remind myself – Arzo, Be Yourself! Just be Yourself. Always be Yourself. That's how difficult it is to be yourself in this place.

Zohra   If I had a t-shirt, it would say, 'Don't be yourself. Thank you very much.'

Arzo   See, you don't understand. You're too Afghan to understand. I have a circle around me, like this, this wide - that's my space. But you Afghans, you just can't see it. In America, people can see the circle even though it's invisible.

Zohra   The gossip must stop. You must stop hiding like a mouse caught in a trap.

Arzo   I am not a mouse, not even a little bit.

Zohra   You are not? How interesting. Why not? Have you been out today? Finally left the house to look for a job suited to someone who speaks English? Is that what happened?

Pause

Stop looking at me as if I am a book written in a foreign language.

Arzo   Honestly mother, you know what it feels like to be me right now? I feel like the big bang is about to occur in my head, like my brain is about to explode out of my skull.

Pause

There, you have that look again. You are scaring me, mother.

Zohra   It's because with every minute, you look more and more like a thief who's about to confess. Is there something you want to tell me, Arzo?

Arzo   Yes I do.

Zohra   What is it? Tell me.

Arzo   I am going to make us tea.

Zohra   Tea? Don't make tea. There's absolutely no time for tea.

Arzo   Oh my god! What happened to you? You never say no to tea. You Afghans, there's a war declared and what do you say? Wait, Tea first, then, war.

Zohra   Sit down, Arzo. I have news.

Arzo   What?

Zohra   I had a terrible email today.

Arzo   What email?

Zohra   An email from Mrs Malik.

Arzo   The landlady?

Zohra   Precisely!

Arzo   What does she want?

Zohra   She wants the house tidy; she wants it spotlessly clean and she wants it presentable. She wants it traditional. A traditional Afghan home. What's the time, Arzo?

Arzo   It's five in the afternoon.

Zohra   People are coming in less than an hour. We don't have time. Come on, give me a hand.

Arzo   What people? Why?

Zohra   To inspect the house, what else?

Arzo   To inspect the house?

Zohra   Yes, to inspect the house!

Arzo   But why inspect the house?

Zohra   To see whether they want to rent it.

Arzo   But we rent here.

Zohra   We rented here. Past tense. Rented.

Arzo   Mother, I don't understand.

Zohra   We have less than an hour to clean and tidy the house. Why? Because people are coming to inspect the house. Why are they coming to inspect the house? Because they can afford to pay the rent in dollars.

Arzo   But we've always lived here and we never paid in dollars. We always paid in Afghanis. There never was a problem.

Zohra   Now there's is a problem. A big problem. As big as America. Either we pay in dollars or we lose the house.

Arzo   How can this be, so suddenly?

Zohra   So suddenly? We are the land that invented suddenly. One day you wake up, suddenly the Russians are here. One night you go to bed, suddenly the Americans are here. We're Sudden-istan.

Arzo   But it's just the two of us, two women, alone. We are safe here because people know us. She can't do this to us.

Zohra   It's not her, it's her son and he can and he will.

Arzo   But her son is in Germany!?

Zohra   Not anymore.

Arzo   Suddenly he's back?

Zohra   He is back and he says only fools get rent in Afghanis. Concrete walls mean concrete dollars.

Pause

Arzo, was there an earthquake?

Arzo   An earthquake? No. Why?

Zohra   Look at the painting.

Arzo   Oh that. I moved it. I changed it.

Pause

Why don't you speak to Barbara, mother? She's foreign. She can help.

Zohra   The painting looks wrong. It's upside down. The mountain is at the bottom, the river at the top. The shepherd is floating in the air . . . Why would you do that?

Arzo   That's the point, mother. Art is supposed to make you question reality.

Zohra   But we can't let people see that. They'd think we've gone crazy.

Zohra   Give me a hand. This is supposed to be an Afghan home. The people want it traditional.

Arzo   Why don't you talk to Barbara, mother? She's your boss, she's a foreigner.

Zohra   I sent you to America. Now you speak English. But what do you do with your English? You sit at home and talk to the walls. You know what the walls say? Go out, find a job that pays in dollars.

Arzo   You are avoiding my question, mother.

Zohra   Barbara can't help us. It's too late.

Arzo   Why not?

Zohra   She's pregnant.

Arzo   She's pregnant?

Zohra   Stop repeating my words back to me like a parrot. She's pregnant.

Arzo   But pregnant doesn't mean ill. Why is that a problem?

Zohra   Suddenly she says Afghanistan's too dangerous . . .

Arzo   Oh my god, this is too much! This is too weird. Suddenly the only foreigner who can help us falls pregnant and wants to leave. Suddenly, Mrs Malik's son is back and wants rent in dollars.

Zohra   Suddenly there's a woman called Angelica . . .

Arzo   Angelica?!

Zohra   Why? Do you know her?

Arzo   Mother, I'll bring you tea and then you need to sit down.

Zohra   As if I have time to sit down.

Pause

Suddenly, Miss Angelica arrives fresh from Germany. Every two minutes, she says, 'Was that okay or was that offensive? Did I offend you? I am sorry if I offended you.'

You know what I said? I said, relax, Miss Angelica, it's only culture, it's not a minefield.

Arzo   Oh my god, she's right. It is a minefield. It is a proper, real, badass minefield.

Zohra   Language, Arzo!

Pause

She's supposed to take over from Barbara. Why should she keep me? I don't know English. All I know is mere local languages which is why I get paid in mere local currency. I have a daughter who knows English but what use is that? She's in love with the walls and the windows. She never leaves them.

Arzo   I can't believe all this. Pinch me, mother, I think I am dreaming.

Zohra   *Sound of an object hitting the floor in* **Arzo***'s room*

What was that?

Arzo   What?

Zohra   The bang, what was that? What's in that room, Arzo?

Walks towards **Arzo***'s door*

Enough, I have to check, I have to see with my own eyes.

Arzo   *Stops* **Zohra** *physically*

No, no, no, not my room!

Zohra   I am not listening to you anymore. Look where it's got us? If only you had a job by now, if only you were getting paid in dollars . . . You could have saved us. But as it is . . .

Arzo   Mother . . .

Zohra   I'm going to your room and I am going to check for myself what the noise is. People are coming. What if they think it's a real dog?

Arzo   It is a real dog!

Zohra   What?

Arzo   You can't go in there. There's a real dog in there.

Zohra   You have a dog in your room?

Arzo   Mother, it has only three legs.

Zohra   Since when, Arzo?

Arzo   Since when what?

Zohra   Since when have you been hosting a dog in the house?

Arzo   Dogs are fine, mother. What people say about them, it's all prejudice. Just stupid prejudice.

Zohra   I said since when?

Arzo   Since today.

Zohra   So you have been out today, after all?

Arzo   Please don't kill me but yes, I rescued a dog and the dog is in my room.

Zohra   What else is in that room? It smells funny even from here.

Arzo   A couple of incense tins.

Zohra   Am I right to think that there's also a bunch of pink and yellow balloons in the room?

Arzo   How did you know? That's so weird.

Zohra   I didn't know but now I do.

Arzo   Mother, I swear, when I set out today, I didn't mean this to happen.

Zohra   You finally left the mousetrap. You opened the door and set foot on your ancestral soil?

Arzo   I was looking for a job. I know that's why you sent me to America. Because I wanted to go but also because you wanted me to learn English so I could get a good job.

Zohra   So that if I die tomorrow, you have something that no one can take away from you. A skill that'll feed you.

Arzo   Remember when I told you that not everyone who comes back from America instantly feels like a fish in water?

Zohra   To which I said and I say again, not even fish feel like fish in water but they still try to swim out there.

Arzo   I tried to swim out there, despite the dust, I tried to swim with the dust, into the dust.

Zohra   But instead of finding a job, you ruined a girl and rescued a dog.

Arzo   I didn't ruin her.

Zohra   How much did you pay her for her tins and balloons?

Arzo   It's just junk, mother.

Zohra   And she promised you she'd stop working and she'd start going to school instead.

Arzo   She's only five, mother.

Zohra   She's five and now she's also unemployed. At home, there's a baby brother and that baby brother is not going to get milk tonight.

Pause

We know it's junk but we pretend it's gold. Arzo, it's about dignity, it's about not making them feel like beggars.

Arzo   I felt it was my responsibility. Someone had to do something, mother.

Zohra   You can't make Spring with just one flower. Go get our headscarf. We're going.

Arzo   Going where?

Zohra   To the street to find the girl and give her back what belongs to her. They all must go, the tin, the balloons, the dog!

Arzo   The dog has only three legs. Have mercy!

Zohra   A dog in a Muslim house? Come on, Arzo, we're losing time. They are coming soon.

Arzo   I can't go, mother. I can't show my face to the world.

Zohra   You have a perfectly presentable face and you have no reason not to show it to the world.

Arzo   Oh mother, you don't know half of it.

Zohra   You are giving me a heart attack, Arzo.

Arzo   *Silent*

Zohra   Arzo, there's a reason god has given you a strikingly long tongue. It's to speak. Spell it out.

Arzo   It's been killing me all day.

Zohra   I don't understand who is killing who right now?

Arzo   I blame the man. There was a man. There were other men, too. But he, I blame him. He is to blame!

Zohra   A man, other men, a guilty man? Guilty of what, Arzo?

Arzo, my heart feels like jelly. Just tell me what happened today.

Arzo   There was an email from Barbara.

Zohra   You should have read it right away. What are you waiting for?

Arzo   You are not going to like it, mother.

Zohra   The email is in English?

Arzo   Of course it's in English.

Zohra   Go on, translate. Let me see what you have learned in America.

Arzo   *Picks up her phone and starts translating*

Dear Arzo . . .

Zohra   Skip the niceties, go straight to the painful truth.

Arzo   You are not going to like it, mother.

Zohra   Translate, show me that the pain of sending you to America was not for nothing.

Arzo   Dear Arzo,

Per your mother's request, I sent emails around to all my contacts in Kabul.

to **Zohra**

I didn't know you had done that, mother.

back to email

I just found the perfect position for you.

Zohra   The perfect position!

Arzo   The US embassy is looking for a local liaison officer. It has to be a girl and she has to know English.

Zohra   Keep reading . . . keep reading.

Arzo   I told them, I know the perfect girl for the job. She's just come back from America but really, she's very Afghan. The perfect bridge between the two cultures, so to speak. A straight bridge made of solid stone.

Zohra   Nicely put. No one wants to walk on a wobbly bridge.

Arzo   *reluctantly*

And of course, since you'll be speaking English, they'll pay you in dollars.

Zohra   In dollars! Arzo, I prayed for this. You are going to save us. Read, read . . .

Arzo   I can't. . . .

Zohra   She finished the email like that?

Arzo   Oh mother . . . this is so painful . . .

Zohra   But you must thank God, Arzo. We must celebrate. The perfect job just when we need it most.

Arzo   Listen to this, mother, listen to this . . .

Reads with reluctance

Angelica, my new colleague, says she saw something horrible today. A scandal, a real example of how not to behave.

Zohra   How not to behave is what foreign Afghans do all the time. Must be one of them. Carry on.

Arzo   Maybe not . . . Maybe I shouldn't carry on.

Zohra   Read, read . . .

Arzo   *Swallows*

Angelica said the good news is that she filmed it all.

Zohra   She filmed the scandal?

Arzo   *Pause*

She says she's going to email it to everyone. It's such a good example of how absolutely not to behave with the locals. She'll put it on YouTube. Everyone has to see it. Did you hear that, mother? YouTube. Everyone! How not to behave . . .

Zohra Must be one of those finger wagging Foreign Afghans. One of those who turn up their noses and repudiate . . . Carry on.

Arzo Mother, I've ruined us.

Zohra Nonsense, you've saved us. We can stay here, we can afford the rent.

Arzo No mother, you don't understand. I have ruined us. I'm not going to get the job. There's no chance.

Zohra We have the email, we have it on authority that the job is waiting for you. You should thank god, endless thanks to god!

Arzo How can I thank god when I am sure I am not going to get the job? Listen mother, listen carefully, that thing that Angelica filmed . . .

Zohra That terrible example of how absolutely not to behave with locals?

Arzo That was me!

Zohra What do you mean that was you?

Arzo I am the one who made the scene.

Zohra Arzo, repeat your words just so I know I am not dreaming.

Arzo I was trying to take the dog to the vet. To get it vaccinated. Because that's the excuse, no, for the prejudice against dogs, that they have disease?

There's an American army vet. He's doing it for free.

Zohra You were walking around with the dog *in our neighbourhood* in pursuit of an American vet?

Arzo I did, mother, I kept looking and I got lost. Turned out I've been walking in circles. The neighbourhood's changed, mother. Or maybe I have changed. Anyway, people noticed me. They were laughing at me because of the dog.

Zohra They were laughing at you?

Arzo I felt that they were laughing at me because I was carrying the tins and the balloons and a dog in my arms. I could just imagine what they were thinking.

Zohra   Wait a second, Arzo. How many people were there?

Arzo   I couldn't see a thing, my sunglasses were covered in dust and I was coughing like mad. I just heard the shouts and the jeering and drew my own conclusions.

Zohra   Maybe they were watching football. Maybe they were cheering cricket. What happened then?

Arzo   In America, women walk naked and no-one looks. They walk dogs, and it's normal. Why can't Afghans be like that? What's so strange about a woman with a dog?

Zohra   I'm sure women in America don't walk naked.

What else is there on the film? Can people see your face?

Arzo   Oh, they can see, mother. They can see my mouth and my teeth, too. I was walking and it felt like the jeering was getting closer, louder. I don't know what happened but suddenly, I stopped.

Zohra   Wait a second, Arzo. You are saying you stopped in the middle of the crowd in our very own neighbourhood?

Arzo   This man was suddenly there and he spat.

Zohra   He spat at you?

Arzo   He spat at the ground but I knew it was meant for me. I knew he spat because I was holding a dog and he thought the dog was filthy and an Afghan girl shouldn't hold a filthy dog in her arms.

Zohra   That's in the film? You holding a dog in your arms like a baby?

Arzo   Now that you put it like that, yes.

Zohra   What did you do next, Arzo?

Arzo   I lost it.

Arzo   You lost it?

Arzo   I lunged at him, mother.

Zohra   The film shows you lunging at this man?

Arzo   I lunged at him with everything, the tins, the balloons and the dog, mother. The dog was frightened, mother.

Zohra   Arzo, You have attacked an innocent man with a poor dog frightened out of her skull? Did people see you? Who saw you? Did they recognize you?

Arzo   Oh yes, mother, I made sure they knew.

I said, hey people of the neighbourhood, hey you hypocrites. My name is Arzo Salih and my mother's name is Zohra Salih and my family lived here for decades. *Be yourself. Always be yourself.*

Zohra   You said those exact words and it's in the film? You mentioned my name, too? Oh Arzo, I can't believe my ears.

Arzo   You should have seen his face. All their faces. There was a crowd. They were stunned.

Zohra   A crowd of utterly astonished, speechless men, looking at my daughter who is doing something no Afghan woman has ever done in history: Using a frightened dog to attack innocent people.

Arzo   I said I think my dog is better than all of you put together. You know why? She doesn't gossip, she doesn't make children work on the streets, she always licks herself clean, she minds her own business, and more importantly, she doesn't spit at women.

Zohra   And all of this is on film? Recorded for ever and eternity?

Arzo   It's not just that I ruined our reputation, I lost the perfect job just when we needed it most. What should I do? It's on film.

Long pause. **Zohra** *gathers her scarf*

Zohra   The neighbourhood comes first. We go house to house and apologize to every one right now. Let me text a neighbourhood lady I know. She's good with these things. She can help.

Sound of knocks on the door

Arzo   You go mother, I can't face it.

Zohra   Don't worry, whoever it is, I'll sort it out.

Zohra *exits. In comes* **Mrs. Malik**

Mrs. Malik   Arzo, my child, what's this face? You don't recognize me?

Arzo   Mrs. Malik, you look . . .

Mrs. Malik   Never mind how I look. But look at you. You look so . . . so *natural* . . . May they burn in hell those gossips who say Arzo is hiding in the house because her hair is pink and she has tattoos all over her face.

Arzo   Tattoos all over my face?

Pause

Mrs. Malik, if it's about the story today that you've come.

Mrs. Malik   That's precisely the reason why I am here.

Arzo   Honestly, Mrs. Malik, I don't know where to hide . . .

Mrs. Malik   *Takes a package from her handbag*

It's not exactly the way they bake it in America but I tried to find similar ingredients in our own country. Come on, smell it.

Arzo   *Smells*

You made me an apple pie?

Mrs Malik   You miss America, don't you? Take a bite, tell me what you make of it? Maybe it's even better than the original?

Arzo   But I don't understand, Mrs Malik.

Mrs. Malik   Let me explain. I said to my son, Zohra's daughter is a smart girl. If I explain it to her properly, she'll understand. Right now, there's a misunderstanding. But if I explain . . .

Arzo   Your son?

Mrs. Malik   You see, ten years in Europe, he's not used to our dust. He's been away too long. Over there the air is fresh and the streets so clean, you can lick the streets. I said, dust or no dust, son, never spit in front of a young lady.

Arzo   That was Yusof, your son? He used to tease me when we were kids.

Mrs. Malik   *Enthusiastically*

He swears it was the dust. It got stuck in his throat. He had to spit. Maybe he has dust allergy, who knows. People get dust allergy all the time.

But he understands why you were upset. He says you are right about the dog, too.

Arzo   He is not angry with me?

Mrs. Malik   He sends his apologies.

I told him listen son, I've lived in this neighbourhood all my life. They've been my tenants all my life. Let me deal with it. We'll bake her an apple pie and we properly apologize and rest assured, she'll forgive us.

Arzo   But I am the one who should apologize to Yusof. I went off on him. I'm so embarrassed.

Pause

But . . . Mrs. Malik, can you please tell your son please don't send people to see the house. We'll find a solution.

Mrs. Malik   I don't know what you are talking about, my child.

Arzo   I'm talking about the rent.

Mrs. Malik   But your mother already paid it today.

Arzo   So there's no problem?

Mrs. Malik   What problem?

Listen, don't worry about today. I told your mother, it happens to the best of us. Every family has one of those strange foreign Afghans. After all, we're so international these days. We wear the globe like a pearl around our necks. Oh yes, very international. God bless you, my girl.

Mrs. Malik *exits. In comes* **Zohra**

Arzo   We're not losing the house? There was no problem with Mrs. Malik? You tricked me!

Zohra   You were under an American spell. I had to scare it out of you.

Arzo   If only Angelica hadn't filmed the whole thing . . .

Zohra   She filmed it but I made her delete it.

Arzo   What?

Zohra   She filmed it but I made her erase it.

Arzo   Oh my god, you had already seen it!

Zohra   I said to Angelica, that's my daughter. It's not a cultural minefield, it's just that America has gone a little into her head. It's just a little bit of *reverse culture shock*.

Arzo   But what about the email? Barbara emailed me . . .

Zohra   She typed it in English, but the words, I gave her the words.

Arzo   And Mrs. Malik?

Zohra   She has a son who acted foolishly, I have a daughter who acted foolishly. We had to figure out something to teach the wayward children a lesson the Afghan way.

Arzo   So Mrs. Malik was the neighbourhood lady you texted?

Zohra   Everything had to be planned just like in theatre. I was the TRICKSTER and you were the FOOL!

Arzo   I was a fool?? I was the fool!

Concerned

But then, what is real, mother? Don't tell me the job is not real?

Zohra   The job is the only thing that's real. You are starting tomorrow.

Arzo   What about the dog?

Zohra   We keep her as long as she stays in the yard, but not in the house. We're open-minded but not crazy open-minded.

Arzo   Oh mother, you really mean it?

Zohra   The poor thing has only three legs. She's one of us, a war wounded, a war veteran. *Shows Arzo the palm of her hand*

Here, smell!

Arzo   It's dust . . .

Zohra   But you are no longer coughing?

Arzo   If my American friends heard this story, you know what they'd say? They'd say no way! Afghan moms are savage.

Zohra   Tell them that stories are the best way to learn and we Afghans, we are a nation of story tellers.

END

A Theatre of Tricksters

The Story of the Afghan Comedy 'Dust Allergy'

Commentary by Nushin Arbabzadah

My play, 'Dust Allergy', was inspired by a news story about reverse culture shock.

I recall the report as a fascinating story of cultural confusion, disorientation and paralysis. The young Afghans in the story had returned to Afghanistan after studying in America. On returning home, they discovered that Kabul no longer felt like home. What used to be invisible and, therefore, immaterial – the dust, the noise, and the poverty – was now cast into sharp relief. The once familiar country now felt strange; and the newly perceived reality became unbearable.

The words of one woman struck me in particular because they revealed the sheer depth of her cultural transformation. She was quoted as saying, 'For two weeks I didn't want to go out, it was so horrible'. This sentence became the seed from which my play grew. For in it was formulated the core problem I wanted to explore: that immersion in American culture – a powerful pop culture of sounds, senses, and sentiments – can hold a young person spellbound to the point of paralysis. The challenge in writing my play therefore became how to show that the spell of reverse culture shock can be broken, allowing our protagonist to snap out of her American hypnosis and wholly return home.

Like all traditional cultures, Afghan culture too is a repository of ancestral wisdom contained in proverbs, poetry, and pithy turns of phrases. Afghan theatre, in turn, is an extension of this oral, traditional culture. That's to say: it draws on ancestral wisdom to find solutions to eternal problems in their ever-newer guises.

It turned out that the play's core dramatic problem – how to overcome a paralysing enchantment – was a stock problem in Afghan culture. The young Afghan woman who returned from America was only the 21st century manifestation of the old cultural theme: the casting and breaking of spells. The spell-breaker, in turn, is the archetypal figure of the trickster.

In 'Dust Allergy', the task of breaking the spell falls to the mother. She uses all the tricks of the trickster trade, from sly jokes to playful pranks, breaking the spell of the foreign culture that has possessed her daughter and turned her reality up-side-down. As the drama unfolds, the mother plays a game of illusion – using secrecy and plots, deception and exaggeration – to make her daughter snap out of her American hypnosis.

The spell thus having been broken, the old culture resurfaces to show the beauty of life in Kabul that is hidden from the senses but revealed to the heart. It's the hidden beauty of the warmth and generosity of both motherly and neighbourly love. The kind of beauty that soothes the senses and restores the emotions.

I wanted the play to be both realistic and reconciliatory. To be realistic, American-inspired sentiments had to stay in the protagonist's character in some shape or form after her cycle of transformation. After all, once someone is exposed to a foreign culture, a residue of the abroad always stays within them. In the play, this is shown in the guise of a stray dog that our protagonist secretly adopts and keeps at home in Kabul at the height of her cultural bewitchment. In the end, the spell is broken, but the dog stays. It stays as long as it knows its place, which is the yard but not the rooms. Order is thus restored and general happiness ensured. More than the jokes that move the drama forward, that is the comedy – the commedia in the classical sense – of 'Dust Allergy'.

Notes

1   https://comm.ucla.edu/person/nushin-arbabzadah/
2   For more of Housaini's journalism, see https://www.theguardian.com/global-development/2018/oct/09/afghan-women-still-jailed-alongside-murderers-for-failing-virginity-test and https://www.theguardian.com/global-development/2019/nov/14/what-happens-to-afghanistans-left-behind-women-as-the-taliban-rises There's a more extensive biography for her at https://www.iwmf.org/community/fariba-housaini/
3   Please see the online version for Housaini's pictures of her contributors: https://www.huffpost.com/entry/reverse-culture-shock-afghan-students-who-studied-abroad-return-home_n_595e9a93e4b02e9bdb0b73b1
4   Arbabzadah, *Afghan Rumour Bazaar*, *ibid.*
5   For a summary report of the season, see here: https://drmcclimans.postach.io/post/theatre-project-on-the-front-lines
6   https://mesc.osu.edu/events/shakespeare-among-suicide-bombers-turmoil-theater-modern-afghanistan-nushin-arbabzadah

3

Behind the Blast Wall

Sonali Bhattacharyya

Adapted from a story by Sparghai Basir Aryan

Journalist Sparghai Basir Aryan was born as a refugee in Pakistan, and describes in her piece how she expected not to feel like an outsider any more when her family moved back to Afghanistan after the fall of the Taliban in 2001; she hoped she would be able to experience the free life her mother enjoyed when a secular Communist government was in power. As her report so painfully describes, she was disappointed. In a video interview with photojournalist Joël van Houdt in 2016,[1] Basir describes her childhood ambition to work as a journalist, and the pleasure of participating in *Sahar Speaks*. Now she lives in Germany; her sister, Fanoos, a footballer for the women's national team,[2] is also in exile.

Kabul in 1979 and 2016:
A Mother and Daughter Reflect on Change

Sparghai Basir Aryan, Sahar Speaks/Huffington Post, 22 June 2016

Huffington Post introduction: *In December 1979, the Soviet Union invaded Afghanistan, beginning 36 years of continuous war and conflict. Here, 26-year-old writer Sparghai Basir Aryan compares her life in war-torn, oppressive Kabul with that of her mother, who lived peacefully and enjoyed wearing skirts and no headscarf, something unheard of today. The women have much in common: both studied at Kabul University and worked for Save the Children. But war made their lives dramatically different.*

Sparghai's text (to see the beautiful stills of her with her mother, and her mother when she was young, please look at the online version of the story[3]):

My mother, Ghuncha Basir (her first name means the bud of a flower), 1979

It is my first time in Kabul. The bustling capital is different from my poor village, Qalatak. In the Pashayi language, the name means "a small village." On a map, it's hard to find, hidden among eastern Afghanistan's high mountains.

I'm one of the few girls from Qalatak to attend university. My mother died when I was only 6, but I know she would be proud. My father, one of the most educated men in the village and a former school teacher, can't stop beaming. Neither can I.

I haven't been able to sleep for the past week – I'm excited by everything I want to learn. Because Kabul is more expensive than my village, I am working part time at Save the Children as a nutrition field worker. We go to the outskirts of the city and check children for malnourishment. We give them advice and some biscuits and milk.

The electronic bus system is so interesting! And easy to use. For a village girl, it's all so exciting. The bus driver and cleaners are ladies. They wear tight jeans, and their long straight hair winds down their backs. I love watching them.

I spend most of my days reading books by my favorite Russian author and political activist, Maxim Gorky, at the big, sprawling university library. I've chosen a perfect outfit to wear for the first week of school: a purple skirt that covers my knees and a tight, white, sleeveless blouse. Oh, and how could I forget my purple heels. I'll wear them with no socks.

I am so excited. One day, my daughter will walk on the freshly-cut green grass of this university.

The future is so bright.

My mother, Ghuncha, 2016

It's hard to imagine I had no fear at that time, in the 1970s. Was I so naïve to think that my daughter Sparghai – which means 'spark' in our native Pashto – would follow in my footsteps?

That she would live in a country of opportunity? Not one of restriction?

That she would be able to walk on the same freshly cut green grass that my sandals and high heels grazed? That she would be able to participate in political protests like I had? That she would be able to wear her favorite dress or skirt in public? That she – and I – would live without fear?

How has everything turned out to be the opposite?

I, Sparghai, 2016

When I look out of my window at the University of Kabul, I see big cement walls. They are everywhere. They are in front of government buildings. They are in front of most buildings. They are meant to keep those inside safe and separate from what is on the other side. But how long does it take before walls crush our own sense of identity?

I've never been able to wear a skirt or a dress on the University of Kabul's campus. My mother used to spend days lazing in the green fields of the campus in her jeans. I can only wear jeans in my house. In fact, I'm not allowed to wear anything that shows part of my body. My legs must be totally covered. Every day, I cover my head so nobody sees my hair. Still, I receive disgusting comments from men.

If I wore what my mother wore in the 70s, I'd face serious threats. I could even be killed by some segments of society. This is sadly all too common in my country.

The electronic buses my mother used were destroyed when civil war broke out in Kabul, in 1992. Now, if a woman drives in Kabul, water or Pepsi are thrown at her. That's why women never drive with the windows down.

Like my mother, I too work at Save the Children. But my job is harder than it was for my mom. I research community-based education. There are no preschools in Afghanistan. When I go to the field to conduct research, I wear a long black head and body covering. And still, I receive scornful looks. Eyes tell me I shouldn't be out in public. That I shouldn't be working, that I shouldn't be – period.

As my mom said, it wasn't supposed to turn out like this. Not for a daughter and a country born by fierce struggle, resistance, and a bold fight for freedom.

The night my parents got married, in 1984, fire and bombs lit up the sky. Afghanistan was fighting the Soviet occupation. My mother was a revolutionary. On the night my older sister was born, there was heavy rain. Large, wet drops covered our whole village. She was born near a mountain that would soon be attacked by the Russian military. They named her Saman, the name of that mountain. They had to flee. My parents bundled my sister up and walked through high, treacherous terrain. Eventually they made it to neighboring Pakistan. They soon settled into a refugee camp east of Peshawar city.

In December 1989, I was born in the camp, the fourth of five children. We were so far from the Kabul my mother always talked about. My uncle named me Sparghai, meaning sparks of fire. They wanted me to bring light to our society.

My childhood was tough. I grow up in the muddy houses and dusty streets of the Khewa refugee camp. Before I was born, my mother started The

Naseema Shaheed High School, named after my paternal aunt who was killed by the Russians, resisting their occupation. My mom taught in the school for 20 years and I'm a graduate. Eventually, the Pakistani government destroyed the school and the entire camp, saying that refugees should go back to their country.

When I was a child I didn't know about my country, my homeland and my people. I was introduced to Afghanistan through the words and memories of my mother. In vivid detail, she would sketch the beautiful streets she used to walk in, her interesting classes, all her girlfriends.

But she always used the past tense. I soon realized that the Kabul she was describing no longer exists.

When the U.S. ousted the Taliban from power in Afghanistan, in 2001, I was joyous. Finally, I would see the country my mom had described.

In 2005, when I was only 15, my father took us to Kabul. My eyes almost shattered. Four years had passed since the fall of the Taliban regime, and almost everything lay destroyed. Still, there was hope. Hope that the government would rebuild the hospitals, roads, and schools. A fresh start. That's what we all wanted. While it wasn't the Kabul my mother lived in – her classrooms are now pockmarked with holes from bombs – I fell in love with the mountains surrounding Kabul. They are crammed full of houses. During the velvet night, they appear like light boxes.

Soon, I began university in Kabul, choosing to major in social studies to learn about a country I was still getting to know with my own eyes. It wasn't long before I realized things might not turn out the way we wanted. That peace would still be elusive. That people would still run through the mountains to seek a better life in another country.

For one, the Taliban hadn't really lost power. That means I hear comments like: "God Bless the Taliban! They are great for not letting women out of their homes!"

Then, there's the everyday battle of walking down a street. At all times, you're judged. And when you're a woman, you're judged simply for breathing.

And it's not just the Taliban or conservatism one fears. NATO convoys have large men in black sunglasses brandishing Kalashnikovs.

When I was growing up as a refugee in Pakistan, I was an immigrant, an outsider. Pakistanis would shout "mahajar" at me, which means "the immigrant." I thought those days of feelings like an outsider were behind me when I moved back to my motherland.

But not a day goes by that I don't feel like an outsider, an immigrant to my own country. This is not the country my mom told me about every morning as she made tea, every night as she tucked me into bed.

When will we be able to have the lives we want and not the lives we flee from? When will Afghanistan become my – our – country again? When will I be able to lay in green fields, gazing up at the big sky as if it wants me there?

As originally featured in The Huffington Post

_____

SONALI BHATTACHARYYA

Playwright

Sonali Bhattacharyya is an award-winning playwright and screenwriter whose work for theatre includes *King Troll/The Fawn*, a finalist for the Women's Prize for Playwriting, *Silence* (Tara Theatre and Donmar Warehouse), and *Chasing Hares*,[4] which won the Theatre Uncut Political Playwriting Award in 2021. She says, 'I'm interested in dramatising the people's history, putting characters centre stage who have previously been obscured.'[5]

When Bhattacharyya presented Palindrome Productions with her play, she told us: 'I'd never adapted a piece of journalism before, so it's been really interesting. I had to find the dramatic heart of the story in order to tell it – the big, overarching theme, as well as the conflict.

'I felt a great responsibility to tell Sparghai and Ghuncha's story with as much emotional honesty as possible. That is, not to give a verbatim account of the *Huffington Post* piece, but to be sensitive to the heart and subtext of Sparghai's writing.

'I'm the child of a refugee and an economic migrant, so the themes of having to leave your home to seek safety, and always wanting to return, really chimed. I also strongly identified with the self-mythologising of the characters, as I recognised it from my own family. I mention in the play how important it is to be able to create your own mythology when you've lost everything, in order to maintain your sense of who you are.'[6]

BEHIND THE BLAST WALL: SYNOPSIS

Two fighters who are taking on the Soviet occupation are hiding out in the mountains, waiting for a woman comrade to bring them food. The characters of Ghuncha, mother of Sparghai, and Sparghai herself, introduce themselves; Ghuncha immediately recalls supporting her husband in the mountains, and giving birth to Sparghai there: 'You need to make yourself into a legend just to hang onto your own sense of self', she says. When Sparghai picks up the story, she's eight; they're living in a refugee camp in Pakistan, and her hero is Che Guevara. Ghuncha puts on a purple skirt and high heels to remember being at university in Kabul in 1979; Sparghai's experience of university includes high blast walls. The woman the fighters are expecting is shot and killed near their hiding-place; she turns out to be the much-mythologised Naseema, after whom the school Ghuncha has started in the refugee camp in Pakistan is named. The play ends with a contrapuntal duet between mother and daughter: 'There's no difference between then…/And now… /If I stand tall and pretend to be brave/Then maybe I'll actually become brave/Because there is only Afghanistan/And a possible Afghanistan.'

Behind the Blast Wall

Sonali Bhattacharyya

Performed 15 and 16 October 2017 at Theatre503, London

Actors: Annice Boparai, Rasheeda Ali
Director: Rachel Valentine-Smith

Characters

Revolutionary 1 (R1)
Revolutionary 2 (R2)
Ghuncha *former revolutionary, mother of Sparghai.*
Sparghai *currently a student in Kabul.*
[all played by the same two actors]

Scene One

1980. A small, cramped cave in the Afghan mountains. Two revolutionary fighters sit around a fire

R1   Where is Naseema?

R2   She'll come.

R1   We'll starve to death waiting for her.

R2   She always comes.

R1   She's got scared.

R2   No.

R1   They've got to her.

R2   Naseema doesn't get scared.

R1   They've threatened her family.

R2   . . . She gets scared, but she pays no attention to it. She carries on as if she isn't scared.

R1   What if they've killed her?

Beat. **Revolutionary 2** *has no answer to this.*

Then we'll starve to death out here.

R2   The Diranis have been out here for over two months. They've survived. So will we.

R1   How do you know?

R2   I see their fire, sometimes, late at night.

R1   Where?

Revolutionary 2 *points out into the dark night.*

How do you know it's them?

R2   It's the hideout closest to their camp.

Revolutionary 1 *briefly finds hope in this.*

They've been out here since February.

R1   The Allaiwals are all dead. The Russians found their supply route and blocked it off. They were under siege for three weeks. *They* starved to death.

R2   We'll be like the Diranis.

R1   Or the Allaiwals. . . . There're spies in the village.

R2   Tariq was a spy, but we dealt with him.

R1   You think the Russians would be so stupid to only send Tariq?

Revolutionary 1 *shrugs.* **Revolutionary 2** *shakes his head.*

That idiot.

R2   Who else?

R1   . . . I don't know. That's the problem.

R2   You're being paranoid.

R1   They can't come and spy on us themselves, so they're using our own people to do their dirty work.

R2   Who would do that?

R1   Anyone who needs the money badly enough. . . . Mawan.

R2   Mawan is a spy. .?!

R1   No. I'm saying he *could be.*

R2   Don't go around telling people Mawan is a spy.

R1   I'm *not.*

R2   . . . If there were still spies, we would be dead.

R1   We might be dead.

R2   I'm not dead.

R1   If she doesn't come we are.

They both look out in the cold night.

Scene Two

Sparghai *and* **Ghuncha** *enter. They're dressed in plain black tops and trousers. The actors will play the same characters at different points in their lives, and all other characters.*

Sparghai   Hello. I'm Sparghai.

Ghuncha   I'm Ghuncha. I'm her/ mum.

Sparghai   /I'm her daughter.

Beat.

Ghuncha   We're from Qalatak.

Sparghai   The name means 'small village.'

Beat

Ghuncha   It's a small village.

Sparghai   In Afghanistan. Where we're from we speak Pashto.

Ghuncha   That's what we're speaking now.

They look to one another. Beat.

Sparghai   Anything else?

Ghuncha (*direct address*)   It's 1984. The night of my wedding, fire and bombs light up the sky. My new husband is leading the resistance against Soviet occupation, and I'm now also a revolutionary.

She changes into a loose kurta, then starts to pack a knapsack with vital provisions – a torch, canned food, a bottle of water, matches, etc.

And so our two daughters are born into the resistance. We name them Saman, after the mountain that offers us safety and shelter after the Russian military attack. And Sparghai, meaning 'Spark', because she is our spark of fire, our goodness. She is our hope as we yearn for home, so far away. We're now refugees.

She wraps a baby sling around herself and gently puts her new baby daughter into it.

Sparghai (*to the audience*)   One thing you get good at when everything's taken away from you, is creating your own mythology. You need to make yourself into a legend just to hold onto your sense of self. Ordinary men and women realised they had no choice but to leave behind their lives and take up arms. But that's pretty scary if all you've done before is . . . run a shop. Or . . . teach at an infant school So you come up with an alter ego. A brave one. An . . . *invincible* one. And you tell yourself if there's enough people like you, you can get your country back.

Ghuncha   We know one day these girls will bring light to everyone, young and old, rich and poor, in the new Afghanistan.

Ghuncha *gently takes the baby out, hands it to someone offstage, and takes off the sling.*

Sparghai (*to the audience*)   If you believe in it enough, who knows? Maybe *I am* a spark of fire. So, now I'm eight, and the Khewar refugee camp, east of Peshawar, Pakistan, is my home, my playing field, my battleground. (*to* **Ghuncha**) The local boys call me 'mahajar'.

Ghuncha   Everyone is an immigrant at some point.

Sparghai   Abdul Awan has never left Peshawar.

Ghuncha   . . . Everyone is an immigrant, or the *descendant* of an immigrant.

Sparghai   Abdul Awan's family have lived in Peshawar for generations.

Ghuncha   How do you know?

Sparghai   I looked up his surname. The Awan tribe are indigenous to Khyber Pakhtunkhwa.

Ghuncha *is impressed. Beat.*

Ghuncha   People who never migrate are backwards and ignorant forever.

Sparghai   You want me to tell him that?

Ghuncha   . . . No. Just remember it.

Beat. **Sparghai** *seems satisfied by this.* .

One day we'll go home. This is only temporary. We're more like visitors than immigrants.

Sparghai   Okay, then, I've seen enough. Let's go now.

Ghuncha   . . . Just a little while longer, Sparghai.

Sparghai   I want to meet your friends.

Ghuncha   I know.

Sparghai   I want to see the mountains.

Ghuncha   You will.

Sparghai   I want to see the little homes, lit up like fairy lights.

Ghuncha   Yes, my love. One day. One day.

Sparghai (*direct address*)   My hero is Che Guevara. The perfect combination of brains and bravery. I quote him often as I play with the other kids, precocious, possibly annoying . . . "I am not a liberator. Liberators do not exist. The people liberate themselves." He merges in my mind with the revolutionaries in my family who resisted the Russian occupation. My grandmother, Bibi, my mum and dad, and my aunt Naseema. I want to be as brave as them when I grow up. In my mind they are one and the same.

Ghuncha (*direct address*)   She's restless, fearless, too clever for her own good. Everything is a question. She almost drives me mad with questions. What makes the sun hot? How deep is the ocean? What makes electricity? The other women laugh at me, trying to always answer her. If I don't know I make sure I find out. I want her to know everything. I want to keep our spark lit up, alive. Anything I can do to make life more bearable in this godforsaken waiting room of a place.

Sparghai   Mum tells me all about Kabul, the home I've never been to. At night I dream about the little mountain huts lit up like dollshouses in the night.

Ghuncha   She used to sneak into classes at her older sister's school. You've never seen a child more hungry to learn. When she was four, the principal had to agree to admit her, officially. All the other children in Afghanistan start school when they're seven. That's our Sparghai.

Sparghai   I continue my classes at the school in the refugee camp. And, yes, there's only a school in the refugee camp because my mum has founded one. She teaches me, and all the other kids in the camp.

Scene Three

A young **Sparghai** *enters with three other school kids. They're 8 years old. They each read from a paper prepared for the class.*

Schoolkid 1   If I could write to anyone in the world, I would write to Martin Luther.

Schoolkid 2   If I could write to anyone in the world, I would write to Martin Luther King.

Schoolkid 3   If I could write to anyone in the world, I would write to Arnold Schwarzenegger.

The other three look at her with surprise and disdain. She shrugs.

Sparghai   I was going to write to my mother's favourite author, Maxim Gorky.

Everyone is impressed.

But then I changed my mind. I decided to write to someone else. Someone contemporary. Someone influential. Someone who inspires . . . very strong feelings in us all.

Beat.

I decided to write to Cherie Blair.

Beat. **Sparghai** *clears her throat and presents her report.*

"Cherie Blair read law at the London School of Economics. She even graduated with a first class honours. She came top of her year in her bar exams. She is a successful lawyer, academic, and charitable patron. In 2013 she was appointed Commander of the Order of the British Empire. She is married to Tony Blair, the prime minister of Great Britain. Cherie Blair says Afghan women and girls are meek, and quiet, and do whatever the men tell us to do.

She pauses to let this sink in.

"But now she is going around doing *her husband's* work for him. She is telling his cabinet this war is for *us*. That the bombs that put us in this camp were to help *us*. To make us confident and educated, like women in the West. I would like to write to her, and invite her to visit."

The other schoolkids exit, but **Sparghai** *remains. She turns to the audience. She's now a young adult.* **Ghuncha** *enters.*

(*to the audience*) We return, finally, in 2005, when I'm 15. Within a couple of years I'm a student at Kabul university, just like my mum before me. And . . . Kabul is still Kabul.

Ghuncha   And is not Kabul.

Sparhai   The "spectacular 2001 U.S victory" in Afghanistan has driven out the Taliban forever.

Ghuncha   And the Taliban are still everywhere.

Sparghai   "God bless the Taliban!"

Ghuncha   "Making sure women remember their place!"

Sparghai   Threatening those of us who dare to work.

Ghuncha   Dare to study.

Sparghai   Dare to drive, walk the streets, leave our heads uncovered.

Ghuncha   Who dare to be women. (*pulling on a stylish purple skirt, then high heels*) Now I'm in 1979.

Sparghai (*pulling on a jilbab and then hijab*)   I'm in 2016.

Ghuncha   *My Sharona* is top of the charts. And *Le Freak*.

Spaghai   C'est Chic?

Ghuncha *nods.*

Ghuncha   It's playing everywhere, every shop, every party.

Sparghai   Um . . . We don't have the charts, here. Now.

Ghuncha *shakes her head and laughs wryly. If anyone in the audience laughs,* **Sparghai** *should glare at them.*

Very funny.

Ghuncha   I'm a student at Kabul university.

Sparghai   I'm a student at Kabul university.

Ghuncha   I'm running late and just make the packed bus to uni. I don't have the correct change. Getting off and breaking my fifty afghani note at the snack stand will mean missing the start of my morning lecture . . . The driver waves me on with a smile. We've never met before but she recognises her in me, me in her. Young women like us, driving Afghanistan forward. Her, literally . . . I sit near the back where it's quiet, so I can concentrate on some of the reading for my course. I have my favourite novel with me too, like a lucky talisman. Maxim Gorky's *The Mother*.

Sparghai *tuts loudly.*

Ghuncha   What?

Sparghai   After everything/ they did.

Ghuncha   /Now you know literature/ has nothing to do with that.

Sparghai   /After everything they did?!

Ghuncha   It's got nothing to do with that.

Spaeghai   Soviet propaganda.

Ghuncha   It's a masterpiece of political literature.

Sparghai *remains unconvinced.*

Well, it's possible it's both at once.

Sparghai   I'm late too.

Ghuncha   I wasn't late.

Sparghai   I have to wait for my driver to arrive to pick me up. It's 8.45, and he's still not here. All the buses were destroyed when civil war broke out in 1992. We don't have a car, and even if we did, I'd be spat at or be targeted with missiles of Pepsi and Fanta for daring to drive while female.

Ghuncha   I arrive at campus early. It's a beautiful morning, the breeze full of the scent of freshly cut grass. I sit on it and take off my sandals, sinking my feet into the cool morning dew as I continue to read.

Sparghai   I head straight inside. The campus is surrounded by big cement walls. "Blast walls." They're everywhere, in front of government buildings, in front of most buildings. They're meant to keep us safe inside, separate from what's outside. But how long does it take before these walls crush our sense of who we are? Sometimes I feel like I'm looking in and looking out at the same time.

They look to one another, suddenly far apart across the years. They smile sadly to each other.

I join student protests against the U.S. occupation.

Ghuncha   How can I stop her? I went on every demonstration against the Russians when I was her age.

Sparghai   I have to walk home after one, as the roads have been closed to vehicles for "security reasons". I'm stopped by a NATO patrol van.

The actor playing **Ghuncha** *becomes a* **NATO officer**, *stopping* **Sparghai** *at the side of a road.*

NATO Officer   Think the Taliban would let you go around protesting against them?

Sparghai (*to the audience*)   The American Bill of Rights includes the right to protest. I don't understand – am I supposed to be grateful? (*lying to the* **NATO officer**) I wasn't at the demonstration.

NATO   Stand over here, please.

Sparghai *obediently moves to the side of the road.*

Where are you going?

Sparhai   Home.

NATO   Where have you been?

Sparghai   On . . . campus.

NATO   You work in the kitchen, or something?

Sparghai   I'm a student.

The **NATO officer** *is impressed.*

NATO   You want my advice, just stick to your studies. There was some trouble after the protest – seems like some of your people just miss the chaos. You don't want to get involved in all that.

Sparghai *looks to the audience and rolls her eyes.*

We're peacekeepers, damn it.

Long awkward beat.

Sparghai   . . . Can I go?

NATO   We're here to help you, for fuck's sake. We're here, risking our lives, missing seeing our families, our kids growing up, just to rebuild your hellhole country.

Sparghai (*under her breath*)   So why don't you leave and let us do it ourselves?

He glares at her, hardly able to believe the defiant words came from her.

NATO   What did you say?

Sparghai (*to the audience*)   Why did I say that? Am I an idiot, or something . . . ? (*to the* **NATO officer**) . . . Nothing.

NATO   No. No, you said something. Something very interesting. Please – I'd like to hear it again.

Beat. **Sparghai** *avoids eye contact.*

Sparghai (*to the audience*)   He has a gun. What would Che Guevara do? Take it from him without fear? "Risk my skin to prove my platitudes?"

Beat.

I think about someone else's hero. My mum's. The Mother in the Maxim Gorky novel, when the gendarmes finally come to search her house. She stands as if she's brave, moves as if she's brave, until she actually believes she is brave. (*She straightens her shoulders, stands taller and looks the* **NATO officer** *in the eye*) I said . . . thank you.

The **NATO officer** *nods, still angry.*

(*loudly and confidently*) Thank you for all your help.

NATO   Okay, then. Go on and head straight back. It's not safe out here.

The **NATO officer** *becomes* **Ghuncha** *once again. She goes to speak to the audience, but can't help herself from questioning* **Sparghai** *instead.*

Ghuncha   So you've changed your mind about Gorky?

Sparghai   Don't gloat.

Ghuncha   I'm not. (*Gloating*) I'm just pleased you've finally realised what a profound classic I exposed you to at such a young age.

Sparghai (*to the audience*)   Just a few weeks before, a group of U.S. soldiers got drunk and lost control of their tank. They drove over a small car, killing four students, people just like me. NATO issued an apology, and that was that.

Ghuncha   You did the right thing. You're a woman, you're educated, you work. That's brave enough in Afghanistan today.

Beat.

Sparghai   I work for Save the Children to pay for my university fees, just like my mum did over 37 years ago. The best thing about my job is I learn new things every day, whatever the topic.

Ghuncha *smiles wryly at the audience.*

I'm a field researcher. I go out to poor and remote parts of the country. Places where people haven't ever seen a TV or a mobile phone.

Ghuncha   Kabul is much more expensive than my village, so I have to work to pay for my studies. I'm a nutrition officer for Save the Children. I visit families on the outskirts of Kabul, identifying malnourished children and providing milk and biscuits. The future of our country lies in their dark eyes.

Sparghai   When I started working at the charity I looked up some of my mum's old colleagues, who I'd heard so much about in the stories she used to tell in the camp. But every single one of them left Kabul during the war. It's down to people like me to rebuild the country now. My mum was able to work alone in the field, without a male guard. She was able to wear jeans and shirts – comfortable clothes to do her work in. I have to wear hijab, sometimes full burqa. Some of the families I visit have never seen my face. Even then, some of the men tell me I have no right to be out in public. They think the Taliban are the true leaders of our country.

Ghuncha *changes into more modest clothes.* **Sparghai** *and* **Ghuncha** *are now at home in Kabul, in 2016, after* **Sparghai** *has returned home from work.*

(*to* **Ghuncha**) They said my dad and brothers must all be dead, for me to have to go out to work.

Ghuncha   Only deadbeats and layabouts have time to harass people on the street in the middle of the day.

Sparghai   They said my jeans were too tight. One of them tried to touch me.

Ghuncha   What happened?

Sparghai   I recognised one of them. I sort of know his sister, but I couldn't remember her name.

Ghuncha   Okay . . .

Sparghai   I asked what he'd do if someone treated her like this. What if there was a group of men treating her like this right now? One of the others started to say she was at home with her mum, where she belonged, but the other one went quiet. He told them all they should go.

Ghuncha   Good.

Sparghai   What if they're there again tomorrow?

Ghuncha   They won't bother you again.

Sparghai   What if they do?

Ghuncha   This is why we came back, Sparghai. This is why you go to work. The children don't just need you to feed their stomachs, they need you to feed their minds. Otherwise they'll turn out like these idiots.

Scene Four

The two revolutionaries sit round the now dying embers of the fire. **Revolutionary 2** *is asleep,* **Revolutionary 1** *is on lookout. He stands up, excited, seeing something in the distance. He waves out at someone in the fields, then shakes* **Revolutionary 2** *awake.*

R1   What is it?

R2   She's here. Naseema's here.

Revolutionary 2 *stands up, relieved, but hardly daring to believe it.*

She must have got held up at a checkpoint.

R1   Where?

R2   There!

R1   I can't see her . . .

Revolutionary 1 *grabs his shirt and points forcefully out into the distance.*

R2   *There.*

Revolutionary 2 *spots Naseema and breaks into a relieved grin. He starts to wave at her, relieved and delighted.*

R1   She has food. Thank god, thank god.

R2   Told you she'd come.

Revolutionary 1 *waves to her.*

Naseema! Naseema!

The sound of gunfire.

R1   Get down.

He quickly crouches and hides, and pulls **Revolutionary 2** *down with him.*

R2   No . . . Naseema.

They both look on helplessly as more shots ring out. Naseema is killed.

Naseema . . .

One of the revolutionaries becomes eight-year-old **Sparghai***, who continues her report to the class.*

Sparghai   I would like to write a letter to Cherie Blair from all of us at Naseema Shaheed School.

R1   Naseema. Naseema!

Sparghai   I would like to invite Cherie Blair here to meet with us. I would like to tell her about my dad's cousin, Naseema, who was braver than anyone I have ever met.

R1   She's not dead.

Sparghai   Her body lay in the fields between our village and the mountains for two hours because her family knew the militia snipers were waiting for them to fetch her, so they could shoot them too. That day every member of her family left for the mountains to join the resistance, including her female relatives. And now every child here will graduate from *Naseema Shaheed* school.

R1   She can't be. We have to get her.

Sparghai   And because of this she will never die.

Sparghai *and* **Ghuncha**, *now both young adults, speak to the audience.*

Ghuncha   It's 1979. I sink my bare feet into the freshly cut grass on campus and imagine my daughter following in my footsteps.

Sparghai   It's 2016. I get home from another long day, working under the watchful gaze of numerous eyes, silently telling me I shouldn't be out in public. That I just shouldn't . . . *be*.

Ghuncha   But now, at this moment.

Sparghai   There's no difference between then . . .

Ghuncha   And now.

Sparghai   Between mother.

Ghuncha   And daughter.

Sparghai   The Americans.

Ghuncha   The Russians.

Sparghai   The Taliban.

Ghuncha   My footsteps.

Sparghai   Her footsteps.

Ghuncha   And if I stand tall, and pretend to be brave . . .

Sparghai   Then maybe I'll actually *become* brave.

Ghuncha   Because there is only Afghanistan.

Sparghai   And a possible Afghanistan.

Ghuncha   There are only us Afghans.

Sparghai   Unified.

Ghuncha   At war.

Sparghai   Resisting.

Ghuncha   Continuing.

Sparghai   Knowing one day we'll be free again.

Ghuncha   By our own hands.

BLACKOUT

Interview with Sonali Bhattacharyya about her play

Had you heard of the 'Sahar Speaks' project before you were asked to be involved in this production?

I hadn't heard of it until Steve Harper at Theatre503 first alerted me to the project as he thought I might be a good fit for the stage adaptations. I read the pieces on the site straightaway and was struck by the honesty and bravery of the women journalists. I thought many of the pieces were ripe for a stage adaptation, especially as we don't see feisty, opinionated, educated and politicised Afghan women like this on U.K stages, possibly any stages!

What excited you most about telling this story?

I was excited by the challenge of dramatising what is quite a personal and reflective piece of journalism. Sparghai's writing is full of irony and pathos, as she reflects on the damage the Soviet, Taliban and U.S occupation have wrought on her country. I had to find the dramatic heart of the story in order to tell it – the big, overarching theme, as well as the conflict.

Is there any resonance with any personal experience for you in the story?

Yes – I'm the child of a refugee and an economic migrant, so the themes of having to leave your home to seek safety, and always wanting to return, really chimed. I also strongly identified with the self-mythologising of the characters, as I recognised it from my own family. I mention in the play how important it is to be able to create your own mythology when you've lost everything, in order to maintain your sense of who you are.

Have you ever adapted a real-life account before?

I've never adapted a piece of journalism before, it's been really interesting. I've felt a great responsibility to tell Sparghai and Ghuncha's story with as much emotional honesty as possible. That is, not to give a verbatim account of the *Huffington Post* piece, but to be sensitive to the heart and subtext of Sparghai's writing, and to try to write the surprising, engaging, and enjoyable play her story deserves.

The over-arching theme of all of the stories of the women who have written them is the curtailment or complete embargo on their freedom of speech. Did this affect the way you approached writing the play?

It's why I was keen to be involved in the project – to continue to give these women a voice, and to listen to what they have to say.

What are you most looking forward to about your play being staged?

I always like to experiment with form and how the story is told, so it's always exciting but also nerve-wracking to give my work to a director and actors for the first time.

Has writing this play changed your world view in any way?

I've learned there are many parallels between how some Afghans view their occupiers with how my family viewed the British occupation of India during the Raj. It's reminded me of the unifying nature of anti-imperialism. It was really good to read these women's well-informed, articulate and ultimately hopeful views on this subject.

Notes

1   You can find the interview here: https://vimeo.com/183455503
2   There's a wonderful cartoon of her on her X feed: https://x.com/Fanoosbasir47/status/1853475580424921218
3   https://testkitchen.huffingtonpost.com/saharspeaks/#sparghaibasir/
4   https://www.youngvic.org/whats-on/chasing-hares; and https://www.nickhernbooks.co.uk/chasing-hares
5   For further details, other titles, and news about Bhattacharyya's current work, please see her website: https://www.sonaliwrites.com/news
6   For more of Sonali Bhattacharyya's engaging and revealing interview, see https://www.palindromeproductions.org/single-post/sonali-bhattacharyya-playwright-sahar-speaks-voices-of-women-from-afghansitan [sic]

4

The Place of Shining Light

Yasmin Joseph

Adapted from a story by Zahra Joya

Journalist Zahra Joya trained as a lawyer in Afghanistan, but told me that when she joined the *Sahar Speaks* programme, 'learning about journalism changed my world'. In her June 2016 piece for *Sahar Speaks/Huffington Post*, printed below, Joya said 'My future remains unclear' – but journalism and exile have clarified it. In December 2020, when she was still in Afghanistan, Joya launched the online agency Rukhshana Media, which publishes news stories in English and Persian/Dari 'to give voice, dignity and support to the amazing women of Afghanistan'.[1] In March 2022 Joya was on the cover of TIME Magazine as one of their Women of the Year,[2] and in December that year she was one of the BBC's inspiring 100 Women: 'I believe in the soft power of words', she told the BBC.[3]

The story by Joya that *Huffington Post* published in June 2016 and that we asked playwright Yasmin Joseph to adapt for the stage describes her dressing as a boy so she could go to school. It's a story that catches the imagination – but Joya is not the only girl to have done this in Afghanistan. It's a phenomenon that has a name – *bacha posh*, dressed like a boy. In her book *Afghan Rumour Bazaar*, Nushin Arbabzadah describes how poor families who needed their children to work as street vendors[4] would dress their girls as boys, a 'pretence that stops at puberty', she says, when 'the world of boundless male freedoms is overnight replaced with the invisible chains that mark an Afghan woman's life'.[5] However Jenny Nordberg, researching case histories for her book *The Underground Girls of Kabul*, found several former *bacha posh* who had refused to revert to female behaviour and dress; the father of one of them told Nordberg proudly, 'Maybe she has some of me in her'.[6]

I Dressed Like a Boy So I Could Go to School

Zahra Joya, Sahar Speaks/Huffington Post, 21 June 2016[7]

Life for an Afghan woman is gruelling, like a constant state of war. The country resembles a burning oven, where one can feel the heat of discrimination with every breath.

I want to tell you a story about the hardship that we women face. And sadly, my story is no different from that of many others. We share the same destiny.

I was born in the Waras district in the southern part of Bamyan Province, in 1993. My family's first reaction to my birth was not happiness but sorrow. If I were born a boy, my relatives would have celebrated with an ancient ceremony.

Inside my father's mud house – day in, day out – my family echoed the cries that I let out, matching each tear, while cursing my mother for bringing another woman into this world.

During my childhood, the Taliban ruled Afghanistan. While the militant group didn't have a direct presence in Waras, their laws were implemented and strictly enforced. In my impoverished village, people were concerned with survival, not education – especially not for women or girls.

But they did collectively hire the imam of the local mosque to educate their boys. Two members of my own family, my uncles, studied at a mosque. However, traditional social norms dictated that girls were not allowed in boys' classrooms. On top of that, the Taliban had outright banned girls' schooling. One of my childhood wishes was to study like my uncles. With the help of one of them, I was able to find a way.

But the solution wasn't straightforward. I not only had to change my attitude, but also the clothes that I wore. At the age of 5, I decided to rewrite my destiny.

I became a boy so that I could go to school.

By Western standards, a 5-year-old is an innocent child, but by that age, I had already seen with my own eyes how my mother had suffered, and that brought me closer to adulthood. I had come to believe that if I didn't have access to education, and remained ignorant of my rights, I would face the same fate as my mother, my grandmother and the other women in my village.

My relatives and neighbours didn't react well to my decision. But my young age helped me remain unaffected by the outcry.

This was the path that I had chosen to reach my goal – my last resort. And to me, boys' clothing symbolized hope for a better future. I dressed in characteristic male clothing and changed my name from Zahra to Mohammed.

From my first day at school, I was known as a boy. I knew that if anyone were to uncover my true identity, it would cause a scandal. Though because of my newfound love for education, I was outwardly happy, my innermost struggle continued.

Many Afghan men behave violently. In order to adapt to this all-male environment, I was forced to keep my emotions at bay. For six years, I was forced to go against what felt natural to me; I was not only dressing like a boy, but also speaking and walking like one. For six years, I abandoned Zahra for Mohammed.

In the meantime – despite repeated requests by my family – I refused to wear women's clothing even out of school. The reason for this was that I wanted the day to come when girls would be able to go to school. Maybe on that long-awaited day, I would become a girl once again.

And the time finally came. When I was in 6th grade, the Taliban was overthrown. Schools under President Hamid Karzai reopened their doors to female students. But parents were still terrified of sending their daughters to school. As a result, various organizations started to set up incentive programs to entice families, including food packages.

The first day that I went to school as Zahra, all my friends were shocked. And why wouldn't they be? Curiously, that's when my problems started. Girls wouldn't accept me as one of their own, while the boys mocked me for "changing my gender" overnight. And it took some getting used to.

On the upside, because of my previous years at school, I was ahead of the village girls, who were illiterate. I could read, write and express my views. And so, I continued to pursue my education with fervour until I completed school.

Little did I know that another dark period in my life would follow because my family would not allow me to take university entry exams.

But my father could no longer stand to see my tears. One day he told me that while he couldn't afford my higher education fees, if I were able to provide for myself, I could go to Kabul and continue my studies at a private university.

His permission was my golden ticket. In the spring of 2011, I left Bamiyan for Kabul. On my arrival, I enrolled at the legal studies department of Gawharshad Institute of Higher Education. But this was by no means an end to the challenges that I would face. I was, after all, a rural girl in a big city. On top of that, I had no money. I couldn't even afford the car fare to university, so I would end up travelling long distances on foot. There was also a great sense of isolation. For the first time in my life, I was living alone in a small room with no one to talk to but my own reflection.

But that wasn't long-lasting. I soon met Zahra Yusufi, who was also a long way from home. She too was from the Waras district. This kind and hardworking woman would become someone I gladly call my friend today. Zahra used to work part-time in an office. When she learned of my problems, she was moved and promised to help me out.

I needed her help sooner than I thought I would. The stress of life had finally taken its toll, and my health started to deteriorate. I feared that I'd have to surrender to my illness, Typhoid, and return home to my family. But my greater fear was sharing the same fate as the other girls in my village: ending up married with no real future.

At a time when I felt my most vulnerable, Zahra gave me a glimpse of hope. She helped finance my treatment and promised to get me a job at her office. I felt strong once again, and could continue to not only pursue my education, but also embark upon a career in journalism with Zahra as my mentor.

After four years, I was able to bring my family to Kabul. I wanted my three sisters to have the same opportunities as me. There are times when I want to shout from the rooftop that I'm proud of all my achievements, despite the obstacles that I've faced. But my future remains unclear.

As a woman, I still fear oppression and I'm aware of the red lines that I can't cross because of my gender – whether they have to do with my clothing or my lifestyle. I'm afraid of shaming my family with my laughter or tears in equal measures.

But I live with the hope in my heart that one day I will live a life of my own choosing.

As originally featured in The Huffington Post

YASMIN JOSEPH

Playwright

Playwright and screenwriter Yasmin Joseph says, 'I connected to Zahra Joya's tireless pursuit of her education and the idea of dreaming beyond the limits of her immediate surroundings. Sometimes stepping into your purpose, pursuing personal goals, growth of any kind, can mean becoming a person that friends or even family no longer understand.'[8]

Joseph studied English literature and drama at university, thinking she wanted to be an actor, but says that after a while she 'massively fell out of love with performing and became increasingly intrigued by writing stories I wanted to see'. Joseph was nominated for the *Evening Standard*'s Most Promising Newcomer award in 2019, and in 2020 won the James Tait Black prize for drama for her play *J'Ouvert*.[9] She is the current writer-in-residence at Sister Pictures, is on attachment at the Royal Court Theatre in London, and is developing a script for Disney+.[10] 'My journey to be a writer has not been the simplest,' she told the *Guardian*, 'in that a lot of my most career-defining experiences have been for no money, and it would have been a lot easier to give up.'

But 'stepping into her purpose' in turning Zahra Joya's story into a piece of drama meant, she says, that she was 'constantly aware of the responsibility in telling someone else's lived experience. For this reason, despite the aspects that have been imagined and fictionalised, I endeavoured to stay very true to the text'.[11]

THE PLACE OF SHINING LIGHT: SYNOPSIS

11-year-old Zahra is dressing for school – as a boy. Her mother Anisa says, 'You look just like the boy your father always wanted'. Zahra says, 'You almost sound proud.' As the conversation develops, it emerges that Zahra/Mohammed has hit a boy at school, to defend another boy who was being beaten: 'I begged them to stop, and they called [the beaten boy] . . . a girl, like the word "girl" was filth on their tongue.' As their intense conversation progresses, her mother says, 'Sometimes I walk into a room and see you sitting there and wonder why there's an imposter in our home . . . Promise me that you will always be my girl.' By the end, there's an uneasy reconciliation between mother and daughter, but one that doesn't feel it could last long in the virulent context of Afghanistan.

The Place of Shining Light

Yasmin Joseph

Performed 15 and 16 October 2017 at Theatre503, London

Actors: Nirgarish Khan, Gehane Strehler
Director: Jennifer Bakst

Characters

Zahra   *11, an Afghan girl. Bright, mischievous, innocent.*
Anisa   *32, Zahra's mother. Kind, stern, honest . . . has internalised the immense change in her country.*

1999. Bamyan Province, Afghanistan. War rages beyond the walls of this home, but we see the small trinkets and homely touches of an enforced normalcy. **Zahra** *is readying herself for school. She dresses carefully, meticulously, as if being tested: securing every button, sharpening the crease of every seam, tucking her hair neatly beneath a hat; this is a ritual and should take some time. The shadows gently drape around her.* **Anisa** *enters quietly and watches.*

Anisa   You look like the boy your father always wanted.

Zahra   . . . Strange thing to say.

Anisa   And this family's normal?

Zahra   It's strange because you almost sound proud.

Beat.

Zahra *wrestles with a stubborn curl threatening to reveal her beauty, her mother rushes to her aid with a pin.*

Anisa   You're losing the softness in your face.

Zahra   Papa says it's wisdom.

Anisa   Like those big books are chiselling at your jaw.

Zahra *looks into the mirror with pride. She rushes to her bag and gifts her mother with a piece of paper.*

Anisa   What's this?

Zahra   It says all of our names, and underneath "may God continue to love and protect us."

Zahra *watches her mother intently.* **Anisa** *inspects the paper before placing it into the pocket of her apron.*

Anisa   I asked you to help your sister in the kitchen before you go.

Zahra   I taught her how to do it on her own, she should be fine.

Anisa   So you make the rules now?

Beat.

Zahra   I taught her to save time, so that when I'm not here she won't have to rely on me.

Anisa   And where do you plan on going?

Pause.

Dunya came to see you last night, why did you pretend to be asleep?

Zahra   I had work to do.

Anisa   You used to enjoy seeing her.

Zahra   Things are different now.

Anisa   *You* are different now.

Zahra   Yes, and she always wants to talk about the same things.

Beat.

Anisa   Dunya is a good girl. Listens to her elders, helps the family, says her prayers and tells the truth. There is a lot you could learn from her.

Zahra   Well, she treats me like a teacher.

Anisa   What good is knowledge if we can't share it with the people we love?

Zahra   Numbers, writing, fine . . . But, whenever I talk about the world, she looks at me like I'm telling stories of monsters under the bed.

Anisa   You are *older* than Dunya.

Zahra   Not that much older. It's not an excuse.

Anisa   Don't be rude.

Beat.

Zahra   Once I said that women can fly planes, she just went quiet . . . like I was lying.

Anisa   Maybe she isn't ready for big ideas.

Zahra   I told her that I could run the fastest in my class and she said it was impossible.

Anisa   She isn't like you. She hasn't seen very much.

Zahra   I told her that when you were young you could wear pretty dresses and your hair-

Anisa   –You mustn't do that.

Beat.

Zahra   Mama . . . lately whenever I'm alone I get this feeling in my head. Like it's overflowing and I'm going to drown.

Anisa   You think too much.

Zahra   It's like I'm being chased. And danger's right behind me.

With worry.

What if I bleed soon?

Anisa *looks at* **Zahra** *wishing she had the words to comfort her.*

Zahra   I can't.

Anisa   I know.

Beat.

Zahra   Mama, am I in trouble?

Anisa (*sighs*)   I don't know.

Beat.

Tell me what happened on Thursday.

Pause.

Zahra   *closes up again and begins to pack her bag in deliberate silence.*

Anisa   All those big words you like to use and right now you can't find one of them?

Silence.

Zahra–

Zahra   –Mohammed . . . Please mama.

Anisa   I'm not calling you that in my home.

Beat.

Zahra   Why can't you just do that for me?

Anisa   Because it's not who you are.

Zahra   It's who I *have* to be.

Anisa   That's a choice that you and your father made.

Zahra   Yes, and now for all of our safety we have to follow it through.

Beat.

If I keep answering to Zahra at home, that's how they'll catch me at school.

Pause. **Anisa** *accepts defeat.*

Anisa   . . . *Mohammed.* What happened at school on Thursday?

Pause.

You will answer me.

Zahra   Hamza started it.

Anisa   Hamza isn't in this room right now. I'm talking to my child.

Zahra   He's *so* mean.

Anisa   Boys are born that way. I'm asking what did *you* do?

Zahra   I hit him.

Anisa *is shocked,* **Zahra** *tries to keep cool under the heat of her mother's gaze.*

Anisa *breaks away from the conversation, startled and wordless. She starts to move around the space with anger, busying herself. Sweeping* **Zahra**'s *feet and moving items that* **Zahra** *needs.*

Zahra   . . . Say something.

Beat.

Anisa   You beg to go to school, then behave badly like that? I think it's time to stop all of this.

Zahra   It wasn't my fault.

Anisa   It's gone too far.

Zahra   Mama he deserved it.

Anisa   Zah- Mohammed. Look at me. I don't care what that child did, I didn't raise him, I raised you.

Pause.

Zahra   They were beating Sadi and I wouldn't join in.

Anisa   So, you tell the teacher.

Zahra   I did. He told me I should join in and play, that's how men are made. Then Hamza spat at me.

Anisa   You wipe it off and you come home.

Zahra   He said I should have been a woman, because I'm useless and scared.

Pause. **Anisa** *takes a moment to register what her daughter has just said. She takes a seat. She looks deeply saddened and it's subtly evident that her daughter is surprised by her compassion.*

Anisa   Astaghfirullah, these men are failing our children.

Shakes her head.

Eleven years old and they're talking like *this*?

Beat.

Why do they hit Sadi?

Zahra   Hamza lives beside him and says Sadi likes to help his mother cook.

Anisa   Sadi's mother has a wayward husband, four sons and only two hands, would Hamza rather they starve?

Zahra   It's like Hamza won't stop until he breaks him.

Anisa (*regretfully, for* **Hamza**)   That child has seen a lot.

Zahra   Every day he finds something new.

Anisa   He's seen a lot.

Beat.

Zahra   At first Sadi would fight back, but that would only excite them, they'd wait and take turns pounding him like a rug, and when they couldn't wait it'd be all at once... He finally learned that just lying there took the fun out of it. There was no chase, no worm for the bird. So on Thursday he just lay there, looking at me, his eyes all frosty with tears, blood from his mouth mixing with the dirt.

Recounting this is difficult for **Zahra***, the words don't flow with ease.*

They told me it was my turn, I said . . . I said a word that I can't repeat. I begged them to stop and they called Sadi my sister, told me I was a girl protecting a girl, like the word "girl" was filth on their tongue.

Beat.

Anisa   Tell me the truth Zahra, you have become very close to that boy.

Pause.

Have you told him your secret?

Zahra *is silent. Insolent.*

I *said* have you told him your secret?

Zahra   It's Mohammed. And no. Of course not.

Anisa   Good.

Hesitates, then-

Sadi is a good boy, a gentle boy, but you cannot be friends with him.

Zahra   Mama!

Anisa   If you go back to school you are to leave him alone, do you understand?

Zahra   But mama, he's my only friend?

Anisa   You leave that boy alone or you never go back there. Understood?

Zahra *is very hurt, she fights tears, but through the pain manages to nod in acceptance.*

Anisa   You have to listen to me. For as long as Sadi is different he will be treated badly, and as long as you stand beside him you will also be a target. This is serious . . . On Thursday your teacher began to ask questions.

Zahra (*under her breath*)   That's because he never has the answers . . .

Anisa*'s eyes warn* **Zahra** *that she's toeing a fine line.*

Anisa   He wanted to know why you take these things so personally . . . Your father said he looked at him like he knew.

Zahra   No chance.

Anisa   Do you know what would happen to this family if they found out? Things you couldn't imagine. Things that I wouldn't even want to tell you because despite your efforts to fight it, you are a child. *My* child.

Pause.

Zahra   What did papa say?

Anisa   He said it must be your mother getting into your head at home, that he'd speak to you.

Zahra   So why hasn't he spoken to me?

Anisa   Because he doesn't understand you anymore.

Beat.

Zahra   My teacher is stupid.

Anisa   I told you to watch your mouth.

Beat.

Zahra   He has the key to something that all of his people need, but he holds it like a sword, threatens us with it . . . he gives us knowledge in drips because he knows how quickly we'll outsmart him.

Anisa   You want to mix with men? You need to accept how they abuse power.

Zahra   I'll respect him for as long as he's useful.

Anisa   You'll respect your elders regardless.

Zahra   One day I'll learn more than him and take his job, and on that day I'll come to work a woman. I'll watch the shock on their faces when I read in my real voice. And I'll let girls join the class, and teach boys that it's fine to be kind like Sadi.

Pause.

Anisa *looks at her child, equally afraid and enamoured by her determination.*

Anisa   Go and help your sister.

Zahra   I'd make sure no child went home hungry. Hamza would clean the toilets. I'd lock him in a cupboard and even on the hottest day give him just enough water to keep him alive.

Anisa   So you want to replace one evil with another?

Zahra   Sometimes evil is forgiven when it's done in justice.

Anisa   What are they teaching you in that place? So when godless men trample their boots into these homes, leaving dust in our beds where fathers existed, ripping babies from their mothers in the name "justice" do you think our God forgives them?

Zahra   Maybe.

Anisa   You have an answer for everything but you would learn so much more if you could just be quiet.

Beat.

Your father risked *everything* to send you to school, because you begged him, you pleaded with him.

Zahra   I shouldn't have had to.

Anisa   We had friends and family laugh at us, whisper and snigger in the streets, but he *still* put his pride aside because he thought you could make the world a better place.

Zahra (*pure*)   I would teach you, mama.

Anisa *is wounded by this rare glimpse of her child's innocence. The following is delivered with stern love.*

Anisa   There is nothing that you can teach me that will be of any use.

Zahra *looks at her mother, eager to understand. They are speaking two different languages.*

Can you teach me how to make everything stretch to feed the entire family? Can you teach me how to pack if we need to flee in the middle of the night? How to study every crack in this wall to keep my mind busy until you make it home safe from school every day?

Beat.

Focus on your books and let me be a woman.

Pause.

Zahra   Well if being a woman is hard, then maybe sometimes I feel like one.

Anisa   Well you're not one. Not yet.

Beat.

Zahra   I have eyes, mama. I know what I want. And it isn't this.

Pause.

You compare me to Dunya, to Salma, I wish I was more like them. I wish I could be good like them to make you proud, but I'm not.

Anisa   You do make me proud. But you scare me.

Zahra   I live every day afraid of shaming my family. Every step I take feels like the wrong one. I don't belong anywhere.

Anisa   Zahra, don't speak like that.

Beat.

You have a family and you belong here.

Zahra   I wish I was Mohammed.

Anisa   You are Zahra.

Pause.

Zahra   Then why did God make me this way? Why did God make me feel the way I feel, think the way I think, if he was going to make it wrong? Why did God set me a trap?

Anisa   You stop that.

Zahra   But Mama it's true-

Anisa   –You are a blessing. A blessing from God himself and every time you question him, you block a blessing coming your way.

Pause. The following exchange is delivered like classroom call and response.

Anisa   Where are we from?

Zahra (*reluctantly, as if she's been here many times before*)   Bamyan Province.

Anisa   And what does Bamyan mean?

Zahra   "The place of shining light."

Anisa   And what brought light here for your mother?

Zahra   Me and Salma.

Anisa   And what will your mother do to guard her light?

Zahra   Anything.

Beat.

Anisa   Good. If you forget everything about who you are, just remember that. You came from love, you live in love, you are loved.

Beat.

Your father wanted a boy, I gave him a girl. We tried again, I gave him two girls. Your grandmother, your aunties, they wept, they prayed, and I could never show it but deep inside I was *relieved*. Because the world does not need two of your father. Some days one feels like too much.

Beat. **Zahra** *stifles a smile.*

It took him some time, yes, but he grew to see that he had an eldest daughter with the heart and courage of a lion. You and your sister, I look at you both and in a country that feels so torn, a place where you can feel pain in the air, you remind me that there is still good. You keep me alive. But Zahra . . .

Zahra *looks at her pleadingly.*

Mohammed . . . I had a daughter. You have to leave me something.

Zahra   I'm still your daughter.

Anisa   Evenings, weekends, you need to give your family some time without this mask.

Zahra   It distracts me.

Anisa   You need to give *yourself* some time without this mask or you'll get lost.

Pause.

Zahra   I'll try.

Beat.

Anisa   Sometimes I walk into a room and see you sitting there and wonder why there's an imposter in our home. I have to stop myself from calling out for your father. I say to myself "who is that stranger?" "What is he doing here?" And when you turn around it's always your eyes that let me know first.

Beat.

But when the eyes change . . . and they've been changing lately, I feel like I'm rummaging around in the dark, looking for a piece of me that's been taken.

Pause.

Promise me that you will always be my girl.

Zahra *holds her mother, it isn't a promise, but it's enough. For now.* **Anisa** *dusts* **Zahra***'s shoulders, straightens her collar and passes her bag.*

Go and help your sister, you're already running late.

Zahra   Yes Mama.

Anisa   And hurry home when you're done.

Zahra   Yes Mama.

Anisa   And no fighting today, my little warrior. I mean it. Your father doesn't need the trouble.

Zahra *nods in agreement. Before she leaves she turns to her mother.*

Zahra   Mama when you were young, what did you want?

Anisa *thinks long and hard.*

Anisa   I wanted you . . . you and your sister.

Zahra *is confused by the answer, but comforted all the same. She leaves.* **Anisa** *resumes cleaning. She moves as if a weight has been lifted from her mind and her shoulders.*

After some time she takes the piece of paper that **Zahra** *gifted her from her pocket and reads it over and over again, silently mouthing the words. Finally she holds it to her chest and closes her eyes.*

END

Interview with Yasmin Joseph about her play

What drew you to be part of this project as a playwright?

I believe in marginalised people being orators of their own histories. For this reason I was drawn to the project's focus on empowering Afghan women to occupy space in a male dominated industry, voicing their experiences on their own terms. I also felt that the project had the potential for an amazing legacy: equipping women with skills in journalism that can be passed down and shared.

What excites you most about telling this story?

I was compelled by the story's many layers; after the first read I developed a sense of its dramatic possibilities. Zahra essentially presents two realms of politics: the backdrop of the Taliban regime and its tangible effects for the people of Afghanistan, and the politics of family and the domestic sphere. I was particularly interested in how these concepts had been internalised by the protagonist and how experience had matured her beyond Western measures. At the age of five it took a great deal of bravery and conviction to decide on becoming a boy in order to get an education;

for me this tapped into an interesting dialogue about the autonomy of young women in today's world and also the idea of gender as a construct.

Is there any resonance with any personal experience for you in the story?

I personally connected to Zahra's tireless pursuit of her education and the idea of dreaming beyond the limits of her immediate surroundings. Sometimes stepping into your purpose, pursuing personal goals, growth of any kind, can mean becoming a person that friends or even family no longer understand. Someone that's harder to work out, or box in. This often causes people to project their own fears and limitations on your dreams. I thought it would be powerful to portray Zahra pushing back and resisting the doubts of others.

Have you ever written a play using verbatim text before?

My first experience of using verbatim text was at school during my GCSEs. With my two best friends, I devised a very political piece of drama focusing on war and morality; in it we used snippets and extracts from various news articles. Another piece of work that greatly inspired me was 'Guantanamo – Honour Bound to Defend Freedom' by Victoria Brittain and Gillian Slovo; I read this at university and developed an immense understanding of how verbatim text can be woven and arranged for dramatic effect.

Have the sensitivity of the subject matter and the adaptation of a living person's story in any way changed your process of writing?

Writing this piece, I found myself constantly aware of the responsibility in retelling someone's lived experience. For this reason, despite the aspects that have been imagined and fictionalised, I endeavoured to stay very true to the text.

Zahra tells her story delicately, and the message is sincere. It was important that the characters within my play felt whole and recognisable, as I wanted to retain the heart of her work.

Before writing I listened to Zahra's interview with the BBC to get a sense of her personality and tone. I then went back to the story and broke it into units of action. As a starting exercise I wrote short scenes imagining conversations between characters at each of those given moments and ultimately became most interested in the relationship between Zahra and her mother. I also began to focus on the need to 'keep her emotions at bay' in order to adapt to an all-male environment at school. Throughout the process I tried to revisit findings from my research, facts about Bamyan Province where the story is set, and also accounts from women on life under the Taliban regime. I then had to decide what would be conveyed using subtext and what ideas would find themselves explicitly in the narrative.

The over-arching theme of all of the stories of the women who have written them is the curtailment or complete embargo on their freedom of speech. Do you have any observations to make on this process/ opportunity?

Given the current political climate, I think this is an incredibly powerful time to drown out the noise and listen to the people that society is constantly silencing or speaking over. With that in mind, my role in this project feels more like that of a translator than a storyteller. I'm excited to explore this narrative using a new medium and also to be bridging the gap between two cultures, giving a local audience an insight into Zahra's life and the lives of women like her in Afghanistan.

What are you most looking forward to about the production/your play being staged?

Without giving too much away, my piece will explore gender and form. I'm excited to see how this will be conveyed in the actors' physicality and movement. It will also be interesting to see how a diverse audience will react to this subject matter. I hope it will be possible for the original story-teller to see the show, or to hear her feedback on the script. I'm really grateful to her, Palindrome and Sahar Speaks for sharing this incredible story with me.

Has working on this play changed your world view in any way? If so, how?

I wouldn't say that this experience has changed my world view as such, but it has definitely provided me with a fresh perspective on the politics of Afghanistan and the cultural landscape of the country. It has also sharpened my focus on the importance of women's voices globally, and the power of language as tool for creative expression.

Notes

1   https://rukhshana.com/en/about-rukhshana
2   https://time.com/collection/women-of-the-year/6150546/zahra-joya/; this includes a recording of Angelina Jolie's Zoom conversation with Zahra Joya

3   https://www.bbc.co.uk/news/resources/idt-75af095e-21f7-41b0-9c5f-
    a96a5e0615c1
4   See Pariwash Gouhari's report on the sexual abuse of street vendors, boys as
    well as girls, later in this volume
5   Arbabzadah, *Afghan Rumour Bazaar*, page 97
6   Jenny Nordberg, *The Underground Girls of Kabul: In Search of a Hidden
    Resistance*, Little, Brown, 2014; reviewed here: https://www.wiwip-kcl.com/
    the-underground-girls-of-kabul-in-search-of-a-hidden-resistance-in-
    afghanistan
7   https://www.huffpost.com/entry/sahar-speaks-zahra-joya_n_57693739e4b0fb
    bc8beb9b96
8   https://www.palindromeproductions.org/single-post/2017/09/25/yasmin-
    joseph-playwright-sahar-speaks-voices-of-women-from-afghanistan
9   Read an account of the play's triumphant transfer to the West End, and an
    interview with Yasmin Joseph, here: https://www.theguardian.com/stage/2021/
    apr/27/i-wanted-to-capture-the-joy-jouvert-writer-yasmin-joseph-on-bringing-
    europes-biggest-carnival-to-the-stage
10 For further information, please see https://www.independenttalent.com/
    writers/yasmin-joseph/
11 https://www.palindromeproductions.org/single-post/2017/09/25/yasmin-
    joseph-playwright-sahar-speaks-voices-of-women-from-afghanistan

5

Parwana: They Bear All the Pain

Alia Bano

Adapted from a story by Pariwash Gouhari

For 'On the Front Lines: Performing Afghanistan', our 2019 season at Ohio State University in Columbus, Ohio,[1] we asked London-based playwright Alia Bano to adapt this piece by Pariwash Gouhari.

'I couldn't even scream': survival and abuse inseparable for Kabul children

Pariwash Gouhari, The Guardian, 7 June 2018[2]

Street children are forced to brave violent sexual predators in the Afghan capital as they struggle to earn money.

For 14-year-old Ahmed*, life as a kid on the streets of the Afghan capital has become synonymous with abuse.

His voice calm and unwavering, Ahmed reels off stories of the assaults he has suffered over the years. "One day, a man asked me to buy him a pack of chewing gum. I went out and bought it, and took it back to his house," Ahmed tells me in a dimly-lit apartment he shares with his family. "He then forced me inside his home and raped me." It happened two years ago, but his stories go back to when he was five years old.

After the first time he was sexually assaulted, Ahmed tried to be more careful, avoiding quiet areas and trying not to travel anywhere alone. But one day, when his brothers were not around to protect him, three teenage boys followed him to a Kabul backstreet, and took turns raping him. This became a regular occurrence but he felt he couldn't tell anyone – especially not his family. Ahmed feared his family would be ashamed of him if they knew; he didn't want to be the one who let them down.

Kabul is heaving with street children like Ahmed, impoverished boys and girls who are sent out by their families to work or beg. They snake through the city's congested traffic, trying to clean car windscreens or peddle trinkets. They are often subject to abuse by male drivers, especially taxi drivers.

After nearly 40 years of conflict, poverty and violence are rife in Afghanistan. Since Nato-led troops ended their conflict mission four years ago, the poorly equipped Afghan forces have struggled with an emboldened Taliban and the new task of trying to contain an Islamic State insurgency.

In this environment, education is seen as secondary to earning money. Many children skip school so they can work to support their families. In central Kabul, children as young as three are dotted about the chaotic urban landscape, dwarfed by the enormous mounds of fruit for sale on their wooden crates, or polishing men's shoes.

Lahla, 10, was forced to work on the streets after her father was killed three years ago. Wearing a long dress and plastic purple sandals that had seen better days, Lahla's skin is burned by the sun, evidence of her long days spent on the streets. Her father, a farmer, was killed on his way home when Taliban insurgents and Afghan government troops were locked in a bloody battle. Her meagre earnings from begging support her mother, sister and brother-in-law.

On a recent day in Kabul, Lahla sits near busy restaurants hoping passersby will give her a five or 10 Afghani note, worth about the same value in British pence. She watches as scores of schoolgirls pass by in their black and white uniforms. Lahla has never been to school.

Not long ago, a man promised to give her money if she led him behind the restaurant where she sat. Lahla agreed. There, he began kissing and groping her. She was powerless to stop it. "I was shocked, and my heart was beating so fast. I couldn't even scream, my voice was lost because I was scared if someone saw that this guy, they would blame me," Lalah says. "Afterwards, I felt so sick – I even got sick – but I couldn't tell my mother why."

Approximately 2 million children work on the streets across the country, with 1.2 million of them doing hard labour, according to the Ministry of Labour, Social Affairs, the Martyrs and Disabled. While the majority work in Kabul, street children also work in large cities across the country, including Herat in the west and Balkh in the north.

There are no official statistics for how many Afghan street children are abused, but anecdotal evidence and social activists suggest it is rampant.

Zabi, another 14-year-old boy who has spent half his life on the streets selling plastic bags, says he cannot think of a single street child who has not been assaulted. He says taxi drivers, shopkeepers and even male university students are perpetrators. Zabi's eyes filled with tears as he recalled how, four years ago, a group of older boys pushed him in the Kabul river and took turns raping him. Zabi went straight to the police, and the boys were arrested. When Zabi's father discovered what had happened, he blamed Zabi for shaming the family.

"Violence is an accepted form of punishment in most households, and children get used to it," said Najib Akhlaqi, head of the ministry's child protection action network. "The children don't just accept it, they expect it." He says the ministry receives phone calls from concerned passersby on a regular basis. When the network dispatches police to the scene, the children often deny they are harassed, fearful that admitting it could invite more abuse later on.

Under the Elimination of Violence Against Women law, those who abuse women and children are liable for jail terms and cash fines. The children are then taken to social care centres. But rights defenders say the law is not being fully enforced. Akhlaqi says the government is developing a system that will enable coordination with organisations supporting children in Afghanistan. Currently, only 10 organisations work under the government's supervision.

Fayazuddin Amini, from the juvenile detention centre, says most incidents of sexual harassment are not reported. When they are, police pass the case to Afghanistan's attorney general, who ensures criminals are punished according to the Afghan penal code and the juvenile code.

Amini says there are many children under 18 who abuse, rape or sexually harass other children and get sent to juvenile detention and rehabilitation centres by the court. Once these criminals finish their term, the government doesn't keep track of them. Sometimes the Ministry of Education will enrol them back into government-run schools. Although there are no official statistics, there have been many incidences of reoffending.

According to the Ministry of Finance, more than 60 organisations, both national and international, work for children in Afghanistan. Other unregistered groups also operate.

Abdul Baqi Samandar, for example, opens his home to about 300 children to learn crafts and study with the help of 30 teachers. Samandar pays each teacher £30 a month, with donations gathered from friends abroad.

Samandar, who is in his mid-60s, says the only true way to help Afghan children is to educate them – by whatever means necessary. "I don't understand the families who do not let their children get free education," he says.

All names of children have been changed

Pariwash Gouhari is a member of Sahar Speaks, *a programme providing training, mentoring and publishing opportunities for Afghan female journalists.*

As originally featured in The Guardian newspaper

ALIA BANO

Playwright

Alia Bano is a London-based playwright and teacher of Pashtun origin. As a Royal Court Theatre Young Playwright, she had a debut success in 2009 with *Shades*, about trials around dating in the Muslim community ('fresh and witty', said the *Guardian*), and was named 'Most Promising New Playwright' by the *Evening Standard*. Since then she has written *Hens* (2010), produced at the Riverside Theatre in London and filmed for the Sky Arts Channel, *Gap* (2011) for the National Theatre, been published in *Connections: Plays for Young People* (Bloomsbury/Methuen, 2011), written *Buried* (2011), part of the Royal Court's Rough Cuts season, and *Let Them Eat Cake* (Royal Court).[3]

PARWANA: THEY BEAR ALL THE PAIN – SYNOPSIS

The play opens with a wry and delicate duet between 13-year-old Parwana and 9-year-old Zari. Their father has been killed, and to try and support the family they're selling stuff on the streets: 'tissues, plastic bags, chewing gum'. Whenever she gets a chance, Parwana is reading a book. They're interviewed by a westerner, who films them and says, 'What beautiful eyes you have'. A man in a 'mirrored black and gold jacket that glistens in the sun' gives them a wad of cash and says he'll be back the next day; they buy watermelon on the way home, and their mother says their saviour has arrived. But when he comes back the next day, with a second man, they take Parwana into their vehicle and rape her. 'She never speaks or reads again,' says Zari. 'No more stories, Mum – we're too old for those.'

Parwana: They Bear All the Pain

Alia Bano

**Performed 7 October 2019 at Ohio State University;
September 2021, rehearsed reading, Tara Arts, London, UK**

Actors in Ohio: Rithika Gopalakrishnan, Mehek Sheikh
Director: JiRye Lee

Characters

Parwana *a 13-year-old girl.*
Zari   *a 9-year-old girl.*

Two girls playing and laughing . . . one of them steps out

Zari   It seems

Parwana   Seems

Zari   Like a long time ago that we laughed . . . really laughed.

Parwana   Maybe when Kaka (dad) was alive

Zari   That seems like many

Zari/Parwana   Moons /Bombs

Parwana   Bombs ago

Zari   Then our routine was different. We would lay in bed after the crow of the cock

Parwana   You would lay in bed

Zari   I would lay in bed, Parwana would be awake with her book, that was before . . . before . . . but I'll get to that later when the story demands it . . . but now we are in a time, at the beginning, where the naivety of childhood protected us from the true horrors . . . the true horrors . . . greater than hunger and thirst.

Where did I stop?

Parwana   You would lay in bed after the crow of the cock

Zari   I would lay in bed, Parwana would be awake with her book

Parwana   Trying to read

Zari   Trying to read

Parwana   I was only 5 but still better than you

Zari   Sitting there like a puzzle that needed solving. I just wanted to dream before I had to cook breakfast before going to school

Parwana   In those days there was a school

Zari   In those days Kaka was alive

Parwana   And while we drank tea

Zari   Slowly

Parwana   Savouring

Zari   And had paratha slowly

Parwana   Savouring

Zari   He would tell us how he was saving to go beyond the border, to a better life

Parwana   For a better day

Zari   Where there was food. . . . Mangoes

Parwana   Watermelons . . . lots of watermelons

Zari   And jobs in abundance

Parwana   We would be safe

Zari   In those days we were alive with hope

Parwana   But hope is an arid desert here

Zari   Parwana would listen wide eyed

Parwana   That's when I believed in stories

Zari   In those days Parwana wanted to be a story teller

Parwana   Like Kaka

Zari   To sing stories like father who would entertain us with tales when he came home from work

Parwana   And sing stories from the Shahnameh

Zari   The Shahnameh . . . the Book of Kings . . . one of the greatest literary works. Written in the Ghazni province of Afghanistan, a book that has lived through many centuries . . . where though Rastum, the hero dies . . .

Parwana always wanted to sing

Parwana   But I would always forget the words or muddle the stories

Zari   So, one day, father brought home a book . . .

Parwana   Our second book . . . another Qu'ran?

Zari   But it wasn't . . . it was the Shahnameh, The Book of Kings, in our home, in all its fine glory

Parwana   The letters danced on the page like beautiful strangers waiting to become friends

Zari   Kaka said . . . Kaka said (*getting distressed*)

Parwana (*hugs her*)   Daughter, one day you will read this and you will never have to worry about not remembering the words. This book will tell you them even when I am not here

Parwana   I fell in love with the book, the miniature picture of Kings, the adventures of Rastum and the women he met in the Shahnameh. I, so, wanted to read it. I turned to Kaka and said one day I am going to write a poem

Zari   What would you call it?

Parwana   The Shahbanu nameh

Zari   The Shahbanu nameh

Parwana   The Book of Queens

Zari   Why not? Kaka said as he laughed and ruffled Parwana's hair. I still remember that laugh. . . . A laugh of joy at the tenacity of his daughter . . . a laugh that his daughter had a thought so strange . . . a laugh because he knew . . . he knew

Parwana   I would never write the book

Zari   A girl's destiny was to be a wife

Parwana   The best thing to be for a girl around here

Zari   At 13

Parwana   At 9, at any age

Zari   If you have a husband, you're one of the lucky ones

Parwana   *Ohbeh*[4] was one of the lucky ones, she had a man to provide for her

Zari   But that all exploded with the bombs.

Parwana   Maybe I'd have written the Shahbanu nameh if that had never happened. Maybe we could have become queens

Zari   But that wasn't our destiny, it probably would never have been our destiny, but for a little while, while we had Kaka, sang, played, danced . . .

Parwana   And went to school

Zari   But the war meant . . . the war . . .

Parwana   It made slaves out of 3 millions different Zari's and Parwana's . . . boys and girls . . . making bricks, selling plastic, tissues, sewing, digging, farming

Zari   If they were born somewhere else

Parwana   On a different line in the map

Zari   They'd be singing Disney

Parwana   Eating hotdogs

Zari   Walking on Nike air

Parwana   The war was meant to save us

Zari   Give us the right to play

Parwana   To school

Zari   To protection

Parwana   To food

Zari   But those are for other children

Parwana   In lands far far away

Zari   Where their ordinary lives are lives we wait for in heaven

Parwana   Our fairy tales

Zari   Those are the places that have set the rules for what is to occur

Parwana   Gods playing with a map

Zari   A great game. A game that needs pawns

Parwana   Many pawns

Zari   Because it's always them

Parwana   the pawns

Zari   the innocent

Parwana   men

Zari   women

Parwana   boys

Zari   girls

Parwana   Zari

Zari   That bear all the pain

Parwana   We bear all the pain

Zari   Again and again . . . if we had not had enough more was coming

Parwana   No warning

Zari   Portents

Parwana   The sun still shone

Zari   I woke up reluctantly and brewed the tea and paratha with my mother for breakfast before the call to prayer. My father gets ready to work . . . poor but proud to be working . . . not begging . . . feeding his family. My father wants us to join him but mother wants us to learn . . . mother is pregnant and father doesn't like to upset her so we were sent to school

Parwana   If fairy tales were allowed here, we would have used the feather of the simurgh[5] to save father

Zari   The belief was that the feather makes the one who holds it immune to all but the hottest of flames. It saved the life of the one in need

Parwana   Just as it saved Zai's wife Rubadeh's life from childbirth in the Shahnameh

Zari   But this is where fairy tales come to die. The graveyard of Empires. He should have been safe. There was an army protecting the city. Not one

Parwana   but two armies

Zari   Ours

Parwana   and theirs

Zari   Large enough to protect a King

Parwana   Or a Queen

Zari   But they couldn't save him, a bomb dropped on him

Parwana   Except here the bomb didn't fall from the sky

Zari   It arose from the chest of another man

Parwana   Like a dragon breathing fire

Zari   A phoenix rising from the flames. (*beat*) He extinguished baba

Parwana   And he extinguished us

Zari   Mother's wails were stronger than the songs of the siren . . . how she cried to God

Parwana   But no tears could bring him back

Zari   At least with Kaka there was food

Parwana   And school

Zari   But that stopped that day. Mother was pregnant . . . her belly as ripe as. She couldn't work. At first we begged to carry on going to school. . . . Parwana still carried her books, her dreams but that stopped when we went hungry. So we begged, there were so many like us, a chorus of children singing our hunger. It was a kind lady who gave us a few Afghanis

Parwana   20 cents or 30 pence

Zari   It was Iqbal, who told us to speak to the grocer. A child like our self, somewhere else he'd become an entrepreneur, here he would always be poor. Buy some things to sell he said. So we did

Parwana   Tissues, plastic bags, chewing gum

Zari   We went to the market selling, and when we were tired Parwana would get out her book

Parwana   What are you doing with that?

Zari   The other children would ask

Parwana   I am learning to read

Zari   Well you won't have time to read much, if you want to make some money . . . but we could still dream then . . . a little. We returned home that day with 5 Afghanis each

Parwana   A fortune

Zari   Then our routine changed, we still rose before the cockerel crowed, and Parwana still looked at her book but now we sold . . . Plastic bags . . . plastic bags

Parwana   Tissues, sir, tissues

Zari   Walking, walking . . . selling

Parwana   From dusk till dawn

Zari   If all that walking and talking were letters in a book

Parwana   We could have easily written the epic Shahbanu nameh

Zari   But history silences us

Parwana   The present silences us

Zari   The Powers that be silence us

Parwana   While the roars of the markets and cars surround us . . . men shout from their cars

Zari   "Move you nuisance"

Parwana   "Go away, girl. Don't block the road"

Zari   "No, no we don't want any tissues." But we ignored these cries, the pushing, the shoving, the dust flying into our faces as the cars zoom off to worlds we cannot imagine. But we can't disappear, we can't go home . . . how else would we eat? Who else would look after our family?

Parwana   Tired and aching with pain

Zari   We're ready to head home

Parwana   When a vision in white approaches, like an angel.

Zari   She speaks in a language we don't understand

Parwana   Speaks in riddles. But I'm fascinated. She could easily be a Queen in my book

Zari   "I thought children couldn't work till 11" she says to her companion

Parwana   But Rights of Children don't exist here

Zari   To play

Parwana   To learn

Zari   Safety from abuse

Parwana   They belong to other worlds over there

Zari   What beautiful eyes you have and she takes a photo

Parwana   A photo that would perhaps rival another one

Zari   A photo like the one in the National Geographic, a photo that shows the plight of

Parwana   the suffering

Zari   of the Afghan child deep in her piercing green eyes. A photo of Sharbat Gula, the Afghan girl, a photo taken in 1985. A photo that makes the world coo and ahh . . . a promise to make futures better

Parwana   Yet there is the same photo again, a different girl with different eyes but the same story

Zari   That photo didn't change anything . . . this photo won't either though hundred will stare at in sympathy and horror it will just become poverty porn

Parwana   All the right noises

Zari   Huffs and puffs

Parwana   But a flaccid outcome

Zari   She holds out a video and a tape. What would you do if you were President? President? This woman is wacko

Parwana   President

Zari   I laugh and shuffle us away . . . but Parwana speaks

Parwana   If I were President I would ensure peace, for the orphans so they could play together and study, and ensure everyone had food for surely this is the role of a leader. I would hold to task those who have ruined this country and make them better. I would ensure everyone could read and write and this way we could send messages to all the people around the world to show them we are their brothers and sisters. I would not eat, or sleep until I knew everyone could do this.

Zari   In that moment I don't see Parwana, I see an Afghan Queen, a President, who should be stamped in history books, or given a chapter in the Shahbanu nameh. But that's just a mirage, for someone screams "genay", girl, girl and my sister begins running to a car to give someone a tissue. Selling paper in exchange for more paper so we can feed a child.

What an incredible child I hear . . . such great footage.

My sister will be someone else's story, someone's else success. How many queens have died in this graveyard of the Empires. The girl with the eyes in the photo . . . . my mother . . . Parwana. We walk home that day and I tease Parwana about her speech . . . President Parwana of the Pashtuns . . . we laugh and giggle . . . we are young again . . . young Queens at least until the cockerel crows. But this game has no need of queens . . . it wants

Parwana   Pawns

Zari   many many pawns

Parwana   men

Zari   women

Parwana   boys

Zari   girls

Parwana   We bear all the pain

Zari   we bear all the pain again and again . . . if we had not had enough more was coming

Parwana   No warning

Zari   Portents

Parwana   The sun still shone

Zari   We wake up before the crow of the cockerel. Parwana is awake . . . trying to read

Parwana   We have tea

Zari   No paratha . . . there isn't enough money and mum and our little brother need it more

Parwana   Still we drink slowly

Zari   Savouring what little we have and then we walk to the market and begin our regular routine

Parwana   Tissues . . . plastic bags . . . chewing gum

Zari   As our throats burn under the sweltering sun and we are ready to leave with our measly earnings . . .

Parwana   he comes out of nowhere

Zari   In a mirrored black and gold jacket that glistens in the sun

Parwana   Tissues he says

Zari   I approach him he looks me up and down . . . I give him a packet. Another he says. I give him another but he beckons to Parwana

Parwana   I walk up to him and give him a tissue . . . he looks me up and down

Zari   These are good tissues he says. Then he gives us a bundle of notes. My eyes bulge . . . I lose my breath . . . more Afghani notes than we had ever seen.

Parwana   10 English pounds

Zari   I will need some plastic bags for my shopping, will you be here tomorrow? I want to say something but I have lost my voice, I nod my head but Parwana speaks

Parwana   Yes sir

Zari   Then I will see you then. We go home early . . . the first day early in a year but just before we stop by the watermelon stall . . . Parwana loves watermelon- it's her chocolate because she has never had chocolate. And we spend some money . . . money of our own before giving it to our mother.

Parwana   And we eat

Zari   And eat

Parwana   Sweet

Zari   Cool

Parwana   Succulent

Zari   And still more money than we have earned in a day . . . a week. All our Eids have come at once and maybe this will mean some meat too. We run home with our prize

Parwana   Our luck

Zari   Treasure like this do not come to people like us. Blessed by God my mother says . . . a gift. She smiles and it's as if all the stars of the night sky have filled our room. A ghost of her former self . . . one of hope and life comes back. You be good to that man she says. He is our saviour, our simurgh she says

Parwana   The simurgh

Zari   Treat him well she says. We think maybe mother is right, because today we play and sing with our little brother . . . our bones not as achy or tired as they usually are

The next day we awake with the crow of the cockerel and we begin to sell

Parwana   Tissues, chewing gum, plastic bags

Zari   Third prayer comes and goes and we think the man has forgotten us. All we hear is

Parwana   "Move you nuisance."

Zari   "Go away, girl. Don't block the road."

Parwana   "No, no we don't want any tissues."

Zari   As the light begins to fade, we stay a few minutes extra . . . not wanting to go home . . . want to see our mother's smile again. Just as we are about to leave a faded red truck pulls out to a stop and there he is but this time there is another man with him. He points to us and the other man nods

Parwana   You're still here. Good, good. Do you have those plastic bags?

Zari   Yes uncle, we do, I say

Parwana   Good, good

Zari   he says but he is not listening to me, he is looking at the man with the beard who shies his head slightly and a message that I cannot understand passes through them. We will take everything you have . . . all of them

Parwana   Everything? All the bags?

Zari   If only we had understood how true he his words were

Parwana   Come bring them to my car

Zari   I get up

Parwana   No not you . . . She can bring them. You stay here, in case someone wants some tissues

Zari   I look at Parwana and she looks at me and I remember mother's words. "Treat him well." Go on go I will wait here, I say.

She walks around the corner with him . . . our saviour and I think of how mother will be pleased and maybe tomorrow we can lie in and have a day off. Maybe I can shop for a new dress and Parwana can look at her book all day instead of snatching a few moments here and there.

A few minutes go by and a few more and Parwana is not back. I begin to worry this is the longest I have been without my sister but I tell myself I am being stupid. I tell myself this a few more times, until I leave the tissues.

I walk towards the corner but I cannot see the man in his black and gold mirrored jacket . . . I walk shouting Parwana . . . Parwana . . . and there next to a faded red truck I see something on the floor, lying in the dust.

It's a book, like the finger worn book that Parwana always carries but it's on the floor. There and not in her bag. I run towards it and pick it up . . . why would she drop it?

I look around I see a glimpse of a black and red jacket moving up and down in the back of a faded red truck. I run towards it but I can't move. . . . The man is there, with the second one and he is on top of Parwana . . . I can hear Parwana crying . . . I can hear a slap. . . . I try to move but I am scared . . . I just stare until I think he is going to look up and then I run and run back around the corner and start screaming

Tissues, chewing gum at the top of my lungs

But these are not the words I want to say. Sometimes later I don't know how long Parwana returns, her hair is dishevelled and her face red. She holds a few limp notes in her hands.

Parwana, I say but she doesn't answer.

Parwana . . . she hands me the money as if she is holding hot coals and starts running and running. I chase after her with her book. And stop just a few yards from the house.

Parwana I say . . . but I have no words . . . so I give her the one thing I know . . . the one thing that gives her joy . . . I give her . . . her book. I hand it out to her, hoping to comfort her and see her smile . . . but she just looks at me and stares and stares. She takes the book and rips it into a million tiny pieces and she buries all the queens and all the stories she ever has.

She never reads or speaks again. Not even when mother smiles and says, ah he came our saviour and prays for the man. Nor does she speak when she says let's hope he is there tomorrow but only shudders. Mother begins to tell the story of the simurgh then Parwana finally speaks

Parwana   No more stories Ohbeh. We're too old for those.

BLACKOUT

Reflection on her play by Alia Bano

'Parwana: They Bear All the Pain' is inspired by a heart-breaking article by Pariwash Gouhari that focused on child street-sellers selling goods to survive. This struggle to survive exposed the children to acts of violence and sexual abuse. Prior to the Taliban, there were schooling opportunities for boys and girl; however with the latest Taliban insurrection, they have enforced strict restrictions and it is women – and especially women with no male to provide for them – who suffer. They need to survive but finding work is hard and dangerous.

Education is a fundamental right but children in Afghanistan are not guaranteed their right to one, due to instability, poverty and the elimination of that right by the ruling governments. How many Einsteins, Jungs and Shakespeares have been lost in the country due to the many regime changes and instability? If our basic needs are not met, advancement in one's life is rare: we are stuck in a cycle of survival, the situation for the majority of Afghans.

The reference to the Great Game in the play is to root the tale into historical context and remind the audience that the tragedies that have been inflicted upon Afghanistan have been across an age; a suffering in length which the populations of most Western countries have not experienced. Furthermore, it is a reminder that colonialism has a hand in the fate of Afghanistan; thus, the West has responsibility to ensure the stability of and resources for the region.

The redrawing of borders and the Durand Line had an impact on my own ancestral roots, taking my family out of Afghanistan and placing them as Pashtuns living in Pakistan. This redrawing of lines is still an issue today. There is a campaign to reunite the Pashtuns as one community in 'Pasthunwala', a territory independent of Pakistan and Afghanistan. This campaign has led to rebellion and fighting in both countries. A decision made by an external force has meant many people have died: there was no real consideration for how the new borders affected the ethnicities and the populations of the countries involved.

'Parwana' is a play close to my heart. I could have been that child if I had been on the other side of the Durand Line. My hopes and dreams could have easily died if my parents had not chosen to travel to England for a better life. With my father passing away when I was nine, there would have been very little my mother could have done to keep us alive, apart from working or sending her kids to work: a reality for many boys and girls. It was only thanks to circumstance that I had access to education and to fulfil my dream of writing.

Often the citizens of Afghanistan are portrayed as uncultured – but this is not the case; there is a great oral tradition and love of stories in Afghanistan. Great writers such as Rumi and Ferdowsi have flourished when circumstances have allowed. That said, most writers today, such as the novelist Khaled Hosseini, have had to flee and find stability before they could weave their power with the pen.

Narratives are crucial to the identity of a people: they reveal what they believe and stand for – but equally how they are perceived. Our first introduction to a nation is often through a written or visual narrative; these are important. Such stories have the power to precipitate change.

Parwana can be viewed as a metaphorical Afghanistan, growing into her power and herself, but stripped of both by external forces. To grow again, she needs support through the trauma. Thus, Parwana's retreat from the world is one of those devastating events: she has lost the one thing that has moved humanity forward.

It is thanks to Zari that her story is told. After experiencing the loss of her sister's voice and power, Zari goes on her own journey. She has an epiphany about the importance of telling stories, of having a voice. Though she believes she can never weave a tale like Parwana, she knows she must speak or something powerful and beautiful will be lost forever.

The play is a rallying cry for individuals and the world to act; to protect the current and future generations of Afghanistan, to give them the life they deserve, and to achieve Parwana's dream of a female Prime Minister one day leading Afghanistan.

Notes

1   For a summary report of the season, see here: https://drmcclimans.postach.io/post/theatre-project-on-the-front-lines
2   https://www.theguardian.com/global-development/2018/jun/07/couldnt-even-scream-survival-abuse-inseparable-kabul-children
3   https://www.theatrevoice.com/audio/playwright-alia-bano-on-hens-and-shades/
4   Their mother
5   A large bird-like creature in Persian mythology that intervenes to save people; its feathers figure in the Shahnameh

Bibliography

Arbabzadah, Nushin (2013). *Afghan Rumour Bazaar: Secret Sub-Cultures, Hidden Worlds and the Everyday Life of the Absurd*. Hurst and Company, London.

Chow, Chin Min Edmund (2016). *Afghan Theatres since 9/11: from and beyond Kabul*. PhD thesis, University of Manchester, https://pure.manchester.ac.uk/ws/portalfiles/portal/54588933/FULL_TEXT.PDF

Chow, Dr Edmund (2019). *Cultural Commodification of Afghanistan: A Case Study of 'The Comedy of Errors' in 2012 London Olympics*, 16 July, https://www.researchgate.net/publication/334524087_Cultural_Commodification_of_Afghanistan_A_Case_Study_of_'The_Comedy_of_Errors'_in_2012_London_Olympics

Ferris-Rotman, Amie (2012). 'Afghan Actors Gear up for a Shakespeare at London Olympics.' Reuters, 27 February.

Ferris-Rotman, Amie (2012). 'Shakespeare Gives Hope to Afghanistan Arts Revival.' Reuters, 6 June.

Griswold, Eliza, translator and presenter, with Seamus Murphy, photographer (2014). *I Am the Beggar of the World: Landays from Contemporary Afghanistan*. Farrar, Strauss and Giroux, New York.

Landrigan, Stephen & Qais Akbar Omar (2012). *Shakespeare in Kabul*. Haus Publishing, London.

Nordberg, Jenny (2014). *The Underground Girls of Kabul: In Search of a Hidden Resistance in Afghanistan*. Little, Brown, New York.